SUMMER DREAMS

2009 Notable Book Tour

D1384864

HU

Summer Dreams

THE STORY OF BOB-LO ISLAND

Patrick Livingston

WAYNE STATE UNIVERSITY PRESS   DETROIT

12 11 10 09 08   5 4 3 2 1

Library of Congress Cataloging-in-Publication Data

Livingston, Patrick.
  Summer dreams : the story of Bob-Lo Island / Patrick Livingston.
      p. cm. — (Great Lakes books)
  Includes bibliographical references and index.
  ISBN-13: 978-0-8143-3365-5 (pbk. : alk. paper)
  ISBN-10: 0-8143-3365-6 (pbk. : alk. paper)
  1. Bob-Lo Amusement Park (Ont.)—History. 2. Bois Blanc Island (Ont.)—History.
I. Title.
  GV1853.4.C22L58 2008
  791.06'8713—dc22
  2007022451

Publication of this book was made possible through the generosity of the Ford R. Bryan Publication Fund.

Designed by Chang Jae Lee
Composed in Scala and Helvetica Neue

Dedicated to my parents, Jack and Hazel, my brothers, Bob, Jim, Walt, and Larry, and my sister, Cathy, who all showed me how to enjoy life both on and off the island.

"Hawaiya, Hawaiya."

<small>Traditional greeting aboard from Joe Short,
aka Captain Bob-lo</small>

Come, leave your work and take a trip with the
CAPTAIN down the majestic Detroit River to the
Great Playground of a Great City, BOB-LO
ISLAND PARK, where cares are forgotten and
life made joyful in the most pleasant
surroundings imaginable.

CONTENTS

ACKNOWLEDGMENTS

When I began work on this book several years ago, I had no idea of the diverse places my research would bring me or of the wonderful people I would meet along the way. The primary research brought me to the Dossin Museum on Belle Isle in Detroit, where curator John Polacsek helped me uncover the treasure of the books of the Detroit, Belle Isle, and Windsor Ferry Company and provided me access to the rich photo archives. Dave Poremba at the Detroit Public Library Burton Historical Collection helped me find the most interesting papers of the Randall Collection. Of equal importance was the discovery of the Marsh Collection—a hidden gem in Amherstburg—where Eleanor Warren and Jennifer MacLeod patiently walked me through the past century of the Amherstburg Echo and beyond. They also pointed me to Fort Malden National Historic Park, where Jennifer's husband, John, helped me look more deeply into the island's past. Among the many local libraries that provided support are the Leddy Collection of the University of Windsor, the Wayne State libraries, and the public libraries of Windsor, Grosse Pointe, and St. Clair Shores, where Cindy Bienieck helped unravel historic mysteries surrounding the island.

At least as important as all of those resources was the assistance the Marsh Collection staff provided in lining up former Bob-lo employees to tell me their stories. The people of Amherstburg who opened their doors to me brought me into a world I was not fully aware of. Not only was I able to get the story from the proverbial horse's mouth; I was able to begin to understand the deep connection that the people of that downriver community have for the island itself. It was at that time that I began considering titling the book *Live from Bob-lo,* because those people were bringing the island to life for me. I was able to begin to see beyond Bob-lo Island as an amusement park and to understand the island as simply going through another phase of its existence.

The individuals of Amherstburg who contributed so much to this story include Pat Warren, Andrew Buckie, Bert and Peggy Cozens, Charlie Bennett, Denise and Dick Bondy, Father Ted Gatfield, Carl Russelo, Jacquie Gibb, Marilyn Robertson, Maynard Hurst, Ted Diesbourg, Tom and Joan Hamilton, Tom Kilgallen, Virginia Barclay, Dona Bondy, Virginia Bondy, and Laurie McCaffrey. On the island itself, I need to recognize the contributions of Gayle Kaess, Dorothy Tresness, Dominic Amicone, John Oram, Bill Rohrer, and John and Diane Pandolfo. In Windsor, I am indebted to Bill Marantette, Elizabeth Thompson, and Herb Colling.

On the other side of the border, I am especially grateful to have been able to conduct interviews with brothers Bill and Ralph Browning, who, along with Chuck Bade, helped me understand the day-to-day work involved in managing the Bob-lo operation during one of its most popular periods. Of equal value were the scrapbooks, photos, and memories of company employees Art and Woody Herrala. Steve Fletcher provided information from the 1940s. Art Carter and Erma Henderson helped me understand Bob-lo from a different perspective. Forester Brian Colter and his sister Nancy Hascall assisted in my research of the origin of bois blanc. Catherine Clapsaddle and Marybeth Vitale provided insights into the life and times of band leader Joe Vitale. Art Woodford and Neal Shine provided much appreciated encouragement along the way. DJ Ronald Taylor brought me back onto the boats at the end of the ride.

Finally, I would like to thank the staff of Wayne State University Press for their efforts in helping to bring this book into the lives of the people for whom Bob-lo Island is so much more than a memory.

My apologies to the people I may have overlooked in these acknowledgments. Bob-lo is such a magnetic attractant that when people heard I was writing this book, they spontaneously began telling me their favorite Bob-lo stories. This book is for you too. Of course, my own favorite Bob-lo stories involve my wife, Janet, who has encouraged me over the many obstacles that are a part of writing a book. You are my sunshine.

SUMMER DREAMS

"ALL ABOARD *for*
BOB=LO = *The Island Paradise*"

For most Windsor and Amherstburg, Ontario, and Detroit, Michigan, area residents, the single word "Bob-lo" initiates a stream of consciousness journey to that one perfect summer day in the park on the enchanted isle at the mouth of the Detroit River. For several generations over the past century, Bob-lo epitomized a place of fun, recreation, and magic for friends and family. As the island park matured, bucolic meadow picnics gave way to dancing and then thrill rides that kept park goers enthralled through many a warm summer's day and night.

Summer Dreams: The Story of Bob-lo Island explores the golden amusement era of Bob-lo Island as well as the island's fascinating history under Indian, French, British, Canadian, and American tourist and residential occupation. In times of both peace and war, Bob-lo Island played a key role and served as witness to the momentous changes taking place in Great Lakes civilization. As the name of the island changed according to the language of the occupants, the use of the island transitioned as well. From Indian campground to British fort to Amherstburg pasture to artists' colony to everyone's amusement park to gated community for the well-to-do of the Detroit suburbs, Bob-lo has served just about everyone sometime in its past.

But serving everyone should not be taken to imply that everyone was served equally. Several groups can claim to have been disenfranchised through Bob-lo's storied past. These include the Indians from whom the island was taken through an alleged British land grab; the U.S. government, who lost Bob-lo because of a questionable cartographic interpretation by the king of the Netherlands; Americans and Canadians of African descent who were denied access to the amusement park because of written and unwritten racist policies; dancers who were forbidden to perform dances considered obscene (for their time) on the boats and in the dance hall; nonteetotalers who were denied the liberty to have a beer on the island; Canadians who were denied access to the island during the Second World War; certain island homeowners who were ostracized for refusing to conform to suburban norms; and the general public who were ultimately denied access to what had been considered an essential part of summer vacation, a

The river route from Detroit and the location of Bob-lo Island. Courtesy Dossin Great Lakes Museum, Detroit, Michigan.

birthright for almost a century. On the plus side, Bob-lo Island served as a critical waypoint on the Underground Railroad for slaves escaping to the free North, and the park itself actually outlived all other Detroit area amusement parks.

While touching on these and other aspects of Bob-lo's history, this book focuses on the island's more immediate past as it transitioned from a private resort to public amusement park. For it is the amusement park that has made Bob-lo unique among the islands of the Detroit River. In early drafts, the subtitle of this book was "A Canadian/American Pursuit of the Business of Pleasure," which was to acknowledge that Bob-lo was an American-owned Canadian island and to substantiate my premise that the park's many successes and failures in the twentieth century were because of the ability or inability of its many owners to adapt to the changing rules of commerce, government policies, and the recreation desires of patrons from both sides of the border. While a succession of U.S.-owned companies managed the island as well as the large steamers *Columbia* and *Ste. Claire,* those who oversaw the day-to-day operation of the park—from superintendents to maintenance staff—were Canadians.

Bob-lo's story as an amusement park reflects the ebb and flow of the North American amusement industry through the twentieth century, with some interesting variations. At the turn of the twentieth century, many urban areas offered park access either by street or railway systems or by ship. Bob-lo's island status and boat-only access was a natural choice for the Detroit, Belle Isle, and Windsor Ferry Company looking to maximize the use of the vessels of its cross-river service to meet the recreation needs of an emerging middle class. But when the Ambassador Bridge and Detroit-Windsor Tunnel made the ferries obsolete in the 1930s and forced the company out of business, new owners saw no option but to continue using the existing transportation system from Detroit to the park. Yet in making that choice, the owners and their many successors opted to engage in a business operation complicated by multiple transportation and government issues that on many occasions brought the operation to the verge of or into bankruptcy. From the demise of the Detroit, Belle Isle, and Windsor Ferry Company in 1938, each of the subsequent owners publicly or privately lamented that the costly operation of the large steamers was a drain on revenues. Almost every owner, frustrated at having to work with several levels of government from two countries because of the boats, explored the possibility of doing away with them and moving the entire operation to Canada. Yet those same American owners were dependent upon the hundreds of thousands of paying customers who rode the steamers from Detroit and were unwilling or unable to envision another way of making the park viable as a Canada-based enterprise. Somewhat ironically, when all other Detroit area parks succumbed to the pressures of urban sprawl, Bob-lo's unique form of transportation helped it to survive. But the boat-only access also limited the park's growth potential, and Bob-lo's latter-day owners could only watch as parks that developed auto access, such as Cedar Point, were able to surge ahead in the market as the amusement park industry revitalized in the 1970s. By the time owners were able to adapt to the realities of the marketplace and make the unpopular changes necessary to save the park, fate intervened and brought the amusement park era of Bob-lo Island to an untimely and unfortunate end.

Summer Dreams is, above all, the story of those people who brought the amusement park to life, those who nurtured it through difficult times, saved it from abandonment, and preserved it for those days and nights when park goers needed the respite, relaxation, and moments of unadulterated fun that Bob-lo had to offer. I have been fortunate to have many of those people tell me, in their own words, their stories of Bob-lo and what it meant to them. They include ride operators, concession stand workers, island police, carnies, superintendents, ship captains and crew, and park owners, as well as customers and island dwellers for whom Bob-lo has had a lasting influence on their own lives and vocations.

Those who knew Bob-lo as patrons knew it as more than an amusement park. They knew it as a place where, beyond the rides, one could explore the distant British-built lighthouse and blockhouse on the south end and clamber about the large white sailors' monument in the middle before disappearing through the undergrowth that concealed the ruins of old mansions on the north end. Bob-lo is a place where lasting lifetime friendships were forged, a landmark and milestone where millions of teens came of age. These people and their stories will keep Bob-lo alive as a vital part of the history of this region and its people.

It is my hope that this book succeeds in helping the reader take another trip to Bob-lo Island—whether from the docks of Detroit, Windsor, Amherstburg, Wyandotte, Gibraltar, or the easy chair—and to again experience what Bob-lo has had to offer the millions of people fortunate enough to have once had the greatest spot on earth in their own backyard.

PREHISTORY–1860

**The formation of the island . . . The island discovered and named . . . The mission
. . . The British occupation . . . Disputed ownership . . . The construction of the
blockhouses and lighthouse . . . The commons . . . The move to privatize . . . The
resort era**

Geologists hypothesize that eons ago, even before the eras of salty seas
and ice, an underground river flowed through the Great Lakes region
and helped shape the channel connecting today's Lakes Huron and
Erie. Divers of the lower Detroit River's Amherstburg Channel near
Bob-lo have identified a stream of frigid water that flows through a
narrow channel along the bottom. Tom Hamilton, a recreational diver
and former Bob-lo policeman, is one of those who wonder if this
stream is a remnant of that preglacial underground river.

The history of Bob-lo Island is as old as that preglacial stream and
the Great Lakes themselves. Bob-lo Island as we know it today was
created from an outcropping of limestone that trapped ocean-bound
silt to create a land mass in the middle of the river. By the time the
first people happened upon the Great Lakes region some ten millen-
nia ago, the island was already in its formative stages.

There is no evidence of people using Bob-lo for anything at all until
the 1600s, when European explorers and missionaries entered the area
and began extensive note-taking of their new world. They recorded an
estimated one hundred thousand Indians living in the region, practic-
ing agriculture to the south and hunting and fishing to the north. The
tribes were small and held territory by force.

The first passage of the island by whites was recorded in 1670,
when two French Sulpician priests, Gallinee and Dollier, led a party of
seven through Lake St. Clair and the Detroit River. Shortly after, parties of French coureurs de bois, noting the profusion of the white-lum-
bered basswood growing there, bestowed upon the island the name
Bois Blanc, which translates to English as "White Wood."[1]

In 1742 Armand de la Richardie, a Jesuit, established a mission for
a village of Wyandot (Huron) Indians on the south end of Bois Blanc.

By 1747 the mission had around three hundred inhabitants housed in thirty-three lodges. Shortly after, the mission was wiped out by a rival band, and the island once again became a neutral ground used for camping by all tribes.[2]

In 1783 the British, having lost the war with the Americans and facing the prospect of being removed from Detroit, began to consider sites for another fort in the area. Bois Blanc was considered prime real estate because it controlled the only deep-water channel at the entrance to the straits, and orders were sent to purchase the island from the local tribes. The British Indian agent Alexander McKee secured the purchase of the island from the Ottawa and Chippewa chiefs but neglected to follow the protocol of a Royal Proclamation stipulating that the land could not be settled until title was purchased by the government from the aboriginal tribes in a public meeting.[3] But the colonial government and British army, eager to establish a foothold on the territory, anticipated royal approval, occupied the island, and erected the first blockhouse in 1786. The colonial government, concerned about the validity of the earlier deed of surrender, initiated a treaty with the Ottawas, Chippewas, Pottawatomis, and Hurons in 1790 and thus obtained, from their perspective, clear title to several surrendered parcels of land, including Bois Blanc.

In 1796 the British, having overstayed their welcome, were finally compelled by the Jay Treaty to leave Fort Lernoult in Detroit. At the same time, the U.S. government formally disputed ownership of Bois Blanc, claiming the island to be in U.S. waters. With possession of the island still in doubt, the British abandoned their Bois Blanc fortress and began construction of Fort Amherstburg across the river.

Bob-lo Profiles: The First Nations

British author Isaac Weld traveled to Bois Blanc on a warm summer night in 1796 as part of his journey through the Americas. His words—especially in the final paragraph—provide insight into the way that the colonial British perceived the spiritual ceremonies of the First Nations.

> *The first night of our arrival at Malden, just as we were retiring to rest, near midnight, we were most agreeably entertained with the sound of Indian music on Bois Blanc Island. Eager to hear more of it and to be witness to their dancing, we procured a boat and immediately crossed the river to the spot where they were assembled. Three*

elderly men, seated under a tree were the principal musicians. One of these beat a small drum, formed of a piece of a hollow tree covered with a skin, and the two others marked time equally with the drum, with rattles formed of dried squashes or gourds filled with peas. At the same time these men sung; indeed they were the leaders of the song which the dancers joined in.

The dancers consisted solely of a party of females, to the number of twenty or thereabouts, who, standing in a circle with their faces inwards and their hands folded around each other's necks, moved, thus lined together, sideways with short steps, round a small fire. The men and women never dance together unless indeed a pretty one be introduced by some young fellow into one of the men's dances which is considered as a very great mark of favor.

After the women had danced for a long time a larger fire was kindled, and the men assembled from different parts of the island, to the number of fifty or sixty, to amuse themselves in their turn. There was a little more variety in their dancing than in that of the women. They first walked round the fire in a large circle, closely, one after another, marking time with short steps to the music: the best dancer was put at their head, and gave the step; he was also the principal singer in the circle.

After having made one round, the step was altered to a wider one, and they began to stamp with great vehemence upon the ground; and every third or fourth round, making little leaps off the ground with both feet, they turned their faces to the fire and bowed their heads, at the same time going on sideways. At last, having made a dozen or two rounds, towards the end of which each one of them had begun to stamp on the ground with inconceivable fury, but more particularly the principal dancer, they all gave a loud shout at once and the dance ended.

In two or three minutes another dance was begun which ended as soon and nearly the same way as each other. There was but little difference in the figures of any of them, and the only material difference in the songs was that in some of them the dancers, instead of singing the whole air, came in simply with responses to the airs sung by the old men. They beckoned to us to join them in their dance which we immediately did, as it was likely to please them, and we remained on the island with them till two or three o'clock in the morning.

There is something inconceivably terrible in the sight of a number of Indians dancing thus round a fire in the depths of thick woods, and the loud shrieks at the end of every dance add greatly to the horror which their first appearance inspires.[4]

In 1811, with the issue of ownership of Bois Blanc still unresolved, the British recruited Indians to help fight the Americans in the War of 1812. Hundreds of Indians bivouacked on Bois Blanc led by chiefs including Black Hawk, Miera, and Tecumseh, who was killed following Commodore Oliver Hazard Perry's victory in Lake Erie. Miera lived to have his name translated and appropriated for the first steam vessel on the Great Lakes, the *Walk in the Water*. That ship anchored off Bob-lo on her maiden voyage to Detroit from Buffalo in 1818.

The Canadian antislavery act of 1793 made the border a point of entry to freedom for escaping slaves, many of whom stayed overnight on Bob-lo before their trip to the Canadian mainland. As a result, there were over one hundred freed American blacks living in Amherstburg by 1828.[5]

In 1831 the king of the Netherlands, as the final arbiter of the dispute over Bois Blanc, awarded the island to the British, and the case of ownership was closed. In 1836 a contract was awarded to John Cook of Detroit for construction of a lighthouse and a stone cottage on the southern end of the island. The lighthouse was built of Kingston limestone and stood forty feet tall with an elevation over water of fifty-seven feet, allowing eighteen miles of visibility. The lamps were lit for the first time that November and tended by the Hackett family until the lighthouse was automated in the late 1920s.[6]

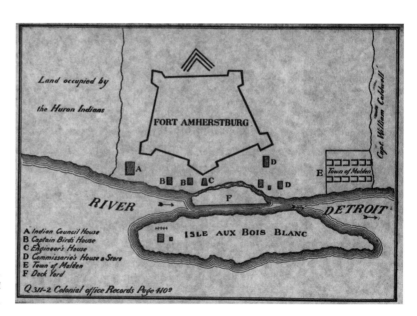

Bob-lo Island circa 1796.
Courtesy Michigan Pioneer and
Historical Society, Washington, DC.

*The lighthouse and keeper's house.
Photograph courtesy Dossin Great Lakes
Museum, Detroit, Michigan.*

Bob-lo Profiles: The Lighthouse

As the lighthouse neared completion, there was much speculation in Amherstburg as to who would secure the position of lighthouse keeper. It ultimately went to Captain James Hackett. An apocryphal anecdote that has acquired folk status relates the circumstances that may have led to his being offered the position:

> *When the lighthouse was built, the Captain's wife suggested that he apply for position of keeper. He demurred, believing he had little chance amongst the strong competition.*
>
> *One day, while his wife was sitting on the veranda with their large St. Bernard dog, she was astonished by the sight of a coach and four driven along the street. The carriage contained Sir Francis Bond Head, Governor of Upper Canada, making a tour of inspection of the district and the lighthouse building.*
>
> *Catching sight of the fine dog, he commanded the coachman to draw up and stop. "That's a fine dog you have, madam," he said. "Very nice indeed," responded Mrs. Hackett. "Is it for sale, madam? I would like to own such an animal."*
>
> *Opportunity knocks but once, and Mrs. Hackett, quick to take advantage of this chance meeting, responded: "No, we had no thought*

of selling him; but my husband is a lake sailor, and he would like to become lighthouse keeper of the lighthouse on Bois Blanc. If you could see your way clear to appoint him, we would gladly make you a present of the dog."

It took just a moment for Sir Francis to say, as his eyes twinkled with delight: "The dog is mine, madam, and the lighthouse position is your husband's."

Mrs. Hackett may have had ample opportunity to regret her decision as her husband supplemented his income as a sailor, leaving her to tend the ambergris oil lights all by herself on the foulest of nights, when they were most in need.[7]

In 1838 a group of Detroit citizens sympathetic to the cause of Canadian independence attempted to capture Amherstburg as part of the Patriot War. Although the attack was repelled, the British determined that they needed new fortifications on Bois Blanc and proceeded to clear-cut much of the wooded area and build three new blockhouses. But after the rebellion was put down and the prospect of renewed hostilities between Britain and the United States had faded, the need for the garrison diminished. Additional acreage was granted to the Hackett family, and a retired sergeant was given a lease of twenty acres on the northwest corner of the island. By 1851, as the last of the British

The south blockhouse.
Photograph courtesy Walter P. Reuther Library, Wayne State University, Detroit, Michigan.

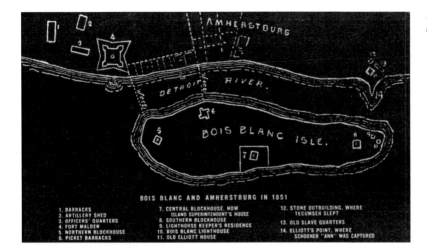

Bois Blanc Island as it appeared in 1851. Courtesy Archives of Ontario.

regulars were being mustered out of the area, the task of maintaining Fort Malden and the island ordnance property, including the block-houses, was given to army pensioners in exchange for housing and land for farming. A visitor to the island at that time described about thirty acres under cultivation by the lighthouse keeper and soldiers, with the rest of the island principally used as pasture for cattle.[8]

THE RESORT ERA, 1861–1892

In 1855, acknowledging the diminishing economic and military value of the island, the Crown decided to focus its attention on more remu-nerative parts of the world and granted control of the ordnance land on the island to the Ministry of the Interior. The entire island, except the lighthouse, was leased to Gordon Macleod in 1861. When he failed to make payments, the island reverted to the government and was sold to Colonel Arthur McKee Rankin, the Amherstburg member of the Canadian parliament, in 1866. Rankin purchased the island, except the lighthouse and ordnance property, for two thousand dollars. Bois Blanc was in private hands.[9]

Colonel Rankin was a distinguished Canadian soldier who helped quell the Patriot Rebellion of 1838. A man of diverse interests, he was also a showman who took a group of Ottawas to Britain in 1843 for a Wild West show. As a fervent antislavery advocate, Rankin later trav-eled to Washington, DC, to offer the services of a Canadian Lancers regiment to President Lincoln at the onset of the U.S. Civil War. He was also a successful entrepreneur who had discovered and held inter-est in the Bruce mining range in the Upper Lakes.[10]

By July 1874 Colonel Rankin had completed a bathhouse with six private apartments on the island. He also intended to erect a number of cottages and a restaurant. He made no charge for use of the grounds by day visitors from the mainland. That September he completed the deal for the ordnance property with the Crown retaining "2 acres for the lighthouse, fishing and fishery rights, all mines of gold and silver and navigable water rights."[11] In April 1875 he appeared before the Amherstburg Town Council with a plan to complete a cross-river railroad that would link the United States to Amherstburg by way of Grosse Ile. He offered to represent Amherstburg on a mission to England to entice investments from the English shareholders of the Southern Railway. At the same meeting, he invited the council and the people of Amherstburg to invest in a Swiss-style hotel and cottages that would accommodate nearly one hundred visitors on Bois Blanc.[12] By June newspapers announced Rankin's plans to place a stock of tents, hammocks, fishing tackle, and rowboats on Bois Blanc Island for the benefit of pleasure seekers. On June 10, 1875, an ad appeared in the *Detroit Free Press* for the sale of village lots five to eight hundred feet deep along the river on Bois Blanc Island.

Rankin's plans for development of Bob-lo as a resort were mirrored by developments both upstream and downstream. Some forty miles north of Bois Blanc, the U.S. government established a navigable channel connecting Lake St. Clair to the St. Clair River and the Upper Lakes. For the first time, ships of up to sixteen feet in draft could make the trip into the Flats. The canal gave a new generation of Detroiters an opportunity to explore the rich St. Clair River delta from a recreational perspective. Shipping companies, most notably the White Star Line and the Detroit and Cleveland Steam Navigation Company (D&C), augmented their port-to-port passenger service by developing hotels and restaurants to serve the public as pleasure resorts along their routes. It now became possible for Detroiters to take an afternoon excursion to places like the Star Island House on Harsens Island, have dinner, and return to the city later the same evening. The success of these places led to development of larger and faster passenger ships, and by the early 1880s the resort era was in full flower throughout the St. Clair River region.[13]

With so much development and attention focused on the St. Clair River, the lower Detroit River remained relatively underutilized from a resort standpoint. The various lines, dominated by the D&C and Cleveland and Buffalo Transit Company (C&B), chose to concentrate their sailings on traveler connections with Toledo, Cleveland, and Buffalo, with an occasional stop in the sleepy little town of Amherstburg.

A White Star Line map of the company's river routes. Courtesy Dossin Great Lakes Museum, Detroit, Michigan.

MAP OF THE WHITE STAR LINE ROUTE

From Toledo, Ohio, through the Maumee River, across Lake Erie, through the Detroit River, across Lake St. Clair, through the U. S. Ship Canal, and the beautiful St. Clair River to Port Huron, Mich., passing many beautiful islands, and the famous St. Clair Flats. A delightful daylight ride of 125 miles; the most charming water trip of the West.

The Lake Erie islands, most notably Put-in-Bay and its mammoth Hotel Victory, were served by ships in transit from one port to another. The Ashley-Dustin Line provided a dedicated service every other day to the islands with the steamer *Frank E. Kirby*. The *Kirby*'s destination was the rail connection in Sandusky, and it did not even make a call at the Cedar Point Resort across the bay.

In the lower Detroit River itself, the smaller Ashley-Dustin steamer *Wyandotte* also made excursion runs to the Sugar Island picnic grounds located between Bois Blanc and Grosse Ile. Sugar Island had been owned by John Clark since 1851, and he had provided excursion service to it on his wooden steamer *Riverside* as part of its Wyandotte, Grosse Ile, and Amherstburg route since that time. In 1876 the Ashley-Dustin Line became the transportation agent for Clark. Interestingly, the philanthropic Clark had no interest in developing the island for the resort trade. His estate stipulated that Sugar Island be kept open to the public and that a passenger steamer service the island.[14] This provision (probably not hindered by Clark's daughter's marriage to Walter Ashley) allowed Ashley-Dustin to build a trade that ferried business, church, and fraternal groups to the island.

Instead of selling the advertised lots on Bois Blanc, Colonel Rankin sold the entire island in 1879 to his son McKee Rankin and his wife, Kitty Blanchard, both noted actors of the American stage. McKee and Kitty, flush with money gained from their work with a successful touring company, ignored the resort scheme and set about establishing a seasonal artists' colony on the island. They built an elaborate gentleman's estate featuring a mansion that incorporated the center blockhouse and became known for entertaining guests from near and afar. They built stables and stocked the grounds with wild game, including deer, wild turkey, elk, and peacocks. A small steam yacht, the *Kitty B,* transported guests to and from Amherstburg.[15] But by 1886 a downturn in business ventures for the stage forced McKee Rankin to place the island and its estates on the market. His situation became more complicated when he fell in love with another actress and Kitty left him and sued for separation. To meet Kitty's demands for reparations, he turned the island property over to her. In 1887 a Detroit paper advertised, "Kate Blanchard Rankin's Subdivision – 317 Villa lots – including Rankin cottage and buildings available at $250 each. . . . The title of the island has been conveyed by Mrs. Rankin to Wm. B. Moran, Comptroller of the City of Detroit who acts as Trustee." The ad showed an illustration of the Rankin house, emphasizing the availability of the ten-thousand-dollar structure with five acres and outbuildings as part of the package.[16]

The Rankin/Atkinson house built around the center blockhouse. Photograph courtesy Marsh Collection Society, Amherstburg, Ontario.

In July the *Amherstburg Echo* reported that McKee Rankin came down on a steam yacht from Detroit accompanied by twenty gentlemen, including Comptroller Moran, several judges, Colonel John Atkinson, and James Randall, who was the architect of the Detroit Boulevard system as well as a prominent criminal attorney. The group was interested in forming a syndicate for purchase of the island, and the *Echo* reported the sale. Instead of being sold to the syndicate, the island, including the Rankin estate and excluding the lighthouse, was purchased jointly by Randall and Atkinson for forty thousand dollars.[17]

The following June the *Echo* reported that Atkinson was ensconced in the old Rankin mansion and that Randall had just moved into his new ten-thousand-dollar dwelling, Lookout Cottage, on the northeast corner of the island. The *Echo* also reported that a work gang was laying out the island with avenues and cross streets and dividing off lots with Osage orange and cedar. Two lots had already been sold on the northwest side, and cottages were under construction, one for J. T. Keena and the other for O. Wardell.[18]

Although they were aware of much of what was transpiring in the St. Clair River area, the new owners of Bois Blanc were slow to further plans for their resort development. Besides their Bois Blanc partnership, Randall and Atkinson were next door neighbors on Detroit's Grand Boulevard and partners in a number of real estate businesses, and they entertained several notable visitors from Ireland, including one John Fitzgerald, president of the Irish National League.[19] Shortly after the island purchase, Randall was encouraged by an 1815 letter written by Lewis Cass, which intimated that the Boundary Commission's recommendation to award Bois Blanc to the British was based on inaccurate information. Excited at the prospect of overturning the

James Randall's Lookout Cottage. Photograph courtesy Marsh Collection Society, Amherstburg, Ontario.

1831 decision, he announced to a group of Irish nationalists gathered at Atkinson's house that he intended to use this information to draw the United States and Britain into a border confrontation that would further the Free Irish cause of establishing Ireland as an independent state. Subsequent research put a quick end to Randall's dream to recapture Bois Blanc for the Americans and Ireland for the Irish. Soon after, he sold his share of the island to Atkinson, maintaining only a few acres on the north end on which Lookout Cottage stood.[20]

Now in almost total control of the island, Atkinson cleared a significant portion for raising oats and millet to feed his stable of forty horses and herd of Jersey cattle. He also constructed a racetrack for his horses. He became locally renowned for his breeding stock, butter, and cream.[21]

In 1893 an ad for rental of Randall's Lookout Cottage for three hundred dollars for the summer offered three stories, ten large rooms, thirteen hundred feet of shore, three acres of ground, and all amenities. Shortly after, the two men had a falling out that affected their business relationship and their social relationship as well. In September 1894 the *Amherstburg Echo* announced that Randall was set to begin construction of two ornate cottages on the island—one for the brewer E. V. Voight and the other for the prosecutor, Mr. Frazer. The cottages would be situated near Randall's and have water drawn from a windmill.[22] After construction had begun, Atkinson claimed that one of the cottages infringed on his property. And, in what was described as "War on Bois Blanc," Atkinson sent a gang of men to the island one night to chop down the offending cottage, resulting in what became known as "Randall's Wreck." A picture of the cottage appeared in Randall's papers with a handwritten inscription: "Two cottages in the course of erection by Mr. Randall. The one on the left destroyed (chopped down) by Mr. Atkinson, a monument to his ungovernable temper."[23]

The matter worked its way slowly through the Canadian courts and was aired by acrimonious letters from the two men each defending themselves through the Detroit newspapers. Finally, in 1900 the courts ruled in favor of Randall, awarding him compensation for the disputed property. But the victory was bittersweet for Randall. Atkinson died before the dispute was settled, and his heirs had already sold his remaining interests to the Detroit, Belle Isle, and Windsor Ferry Company for their new venture on Bois Blanc.[24]

The metamorphosis of Bois Blanc from a resort to a park for the public . . . Steamboat wars for destinations on the rivers . . . The Detroit, Belle Isle, and Windsor Ferry Company joins the competition . . . Bois Blanc is reborn . . . The coming of the *Columbia*

While James Randall and John Atkinson were still in the midst of their property dispute, businesses along other stretches of the river were creating a scenario that would change Bob-lo from a backwater island to a regional destination for the next century. In spite of a nagging recession that began in 1893, or perhaps because of it, change was working its way like a confluence of currents against a soft bank.

While the St. Clair River resorts continued to attract individuals and families to their sites, the Ashley-Dustin Line had successfully developed and marketed day picnic excursions for conventioneer, church, and business groups to Sugar Island and Put-in-Bay. In 1892 they built the larger steel-hulled *Wyandotte* to replace John Clark's *Riverside*, further increasing their market share potential.

In the meantime, the resorts and clubs at the Flats were becoming overwhelmed by the ever-expanding daytrippers from Detroit seeking affordable recreation. These people were ready to do more than have three square meals a day and kick back on the veranda as the previous generation had. The resorts suddenly found themselves competing for the crowds by offering more active forms of recreation, including ball diamonds, drill grounds, dance floors, and bicycle tracks.

To add to the mix, the Detroit, Belle Isle, and Windsor Ferry Company, led by its president, Walter Campbell, was looking to compensate for revenues threatened by potential erosion of its Belle Isle market. Campbell had been one of the original coalition of ferry owners and captains that initiated the Detroit and Windsor Ferry Association in 1877. The association changed ownership a few times over the next decade and changed its name to the Detroit, Belle Isle, and Windsor Ferry Company when it received the tender to provide services to Detroit's new island park in 1879. Campbell and two of his brothers led a group that purchased the assets of the Ferry Company in 1891. But by the mid-1890s competition among several streetcar companies meant there was a real possibility that people would be able to get to Belle Isle directly by street rail without using the ferry.[1] With two new ships, the *Promise* (1892) and the *Pleasure* (1894), built primarily for the Belle Isle run, Campbell and the Ferry Company wasted no time seeking out alternate destinations for those vessels.

Campbell, a hardnosed and savvy businessman, distinguished himself principally through his successful efforts to maintain favorable lease and ticket rates for what in effect was a ferry monopoly between the downtown docks of the cities of Detroit and Windsor. He had no fear of the government representatives who tried to persuade him to give them more favorable rates and successfully parried assaults from political leaders from both sides of the river by simply refusing to give in.[2]

Campbell was politically astute enough to realize that his control did not extend to the streetcar companies competing to serve the citizens of Detroit. And so in 1896, as a new streetcar route bypassed the ferry docks to bring passengers directly to the Belle Isle Bridge, Campbell conceded the loss of revenue and looked upriver to regain it at the already popular Harsens Island. He leased a site on the Algonac-facing shore, named it Beau Voir, and began sending his steamers there on daily excursions. Beau Voir, according to local accounts, featured "baseball and drill grounds, many elm and oak trees and all the accessories of a cool and inviting hot weather resort."[3]

With his response to the streetcar challenge to the Ferry Company's Belle Isle trade, Campbell shook up the river excursion market as well. He sent a signal to the White Star Line that the Harsens Island and St. Clair Flats trade was open for competition and at the same time sent a volley across the bow of the Ashley-Dustin Line for the lucrative and expanding excursion group market.

Not to be outdone, Charles Bielman, the manager of the White Star Line, quickly acquired the Oak Grove picnic grounds in the Flats to compete with the Ferry Company. Bielman's long-term management experience and connections in the Flats area forced Campbell to retreat. The Ferry Company pulled out of Beau Voir by July and finished out the season providing service to Palmleaf, the former Des-Chree-Shos-Ka Hotel grounds on Fighting Island downriver.[4]

But Bielman had more at stake than simply defending the turf of the White Star Line. He was aware of the changing needs of excursionists and worked to meet the demands of that market. An additional White Star destination in the Flats would ensure that the resort crowd would still have service to their favorite hotels, while, on the same run, the new generation would have access to their picnic and recreation grounds for daytrips.

Bielman was confronted by three immediate problems. First, he needed to secure a location: while Oak Grove proved effective in meeting Campbell's challenge, it was only a rented space; he needed to acquire property for long-term development. The second problem related to the prime destination in the Flats—the Star Island House. The house, owned by the White Star Line, had leased access to a privately held dock only through 1900. With the keen competition for destination sites in the Flats, there was no guarantee that the dock to the Star Island House would be available or affordable beyond that year. That reality reinforced the need for a White Star–owned waterfront property. The third problem resulted from the continued growth in popularity of the Flats as an excursion destination. Besides the resort and excursion trade, the White Star Line provided service to several stops between Detroit and Port Huron. The population of Detroit, already beginning to show signs of rapid expansion, meant a larger potential market for their business. Consideration needed to be given to transporting these anticipated thousands back and forth from both Port Huron and the Flats in a rapid manner while still providing more amenities than the competition.

Bielman tackled the first two problems by purchasing a property with dock access just below Sans Souci on Harsens Island. By the summer of 1897 Tashmoo Park opened for business. This set the stage for resolution of the third problem. In early 1899 Bielman commissioned renowned marine architect Frank E. Kirby to design a three-hundred-foot passenger ship that would set a new standard for the Detroit–Port Huron run. In the space of less than two years, Bielman had established the White Star Line as the preeminent transportation in the Detroit area and Tashmoo Park as its top excursion destination. With a new dance hall and pavilion, the park itself almost immediately succeeded in capturing a significant amount of the weekend group excursion business from the status quo service offered by Ashley-Dustin. The new ship promised to win the summer moonlight excursion business from Ashley-Dustin and the Ferry Company as well.[5]

None of this went unnoticed by Campbell. Not one to nurse his wounds, he saw the almost virginal Bois Blanc and began to dicker for a piece of the Atkinson property. By December 1897, months after Tashmoo Park had successfully completed its inaugural season, the next battlefield for the summer excursion crowds was proclaimed. The Ferry Company signed a ten-year lease with Atkinson for twenty-five acres of Bois Blanc Island with the option of buying at the end of that time. The *Detroit Tribune* announced, "A New Park: Bois Blanc Island Selected for It":

The grove of 25 acres will be improved. There will be a dance casino, an observatory, pavilions, bath and boat houses, baseball diamond, bicycle track, lawn tennis courts, and a fine bathing beach, the last of fine sand and free of dangerous eddies.

The Ferry Company proposes to cut a big figure this coming summer. It will book for the new resort down the river and for Walpole Island, Beauvoir and Oak Grove above.

A few days later, the *Detroit Free Press* headlined, "Summer Excursions: Three Detroit Lines to Have Hot Competition for 'Em: Ferry Company, Star Line and Ashley and Dustin in It."[6]

In April 1898 the *Windsor Evening Record* proudly reported that the Ferry Company had used almost all Amherstburg labor and materials for the construction of buildings on the island. The same paper a month later gushed, "The Ferry Company in its endeavors to cater to the public with its usual generosity has spared no expense in this and all other sources of its ample inducements for spending a day of exhilatory, health-giving relaxation. . . . The [dance] casino will be entirely under one roof with its belvedere outlook and flag staffs up by Saturday. . . . This belvedere will be reached by a broad staircase from the level of the dancing floor." Also in place were a boathouse and a bathhouse adjacent the beach on the west side, a cycle track, and a tiled baseball diamond. Flowers were planted throughout the park. Lavatories were situated under the banks, and a main line of sewerage was being installed. Although there was a small power station, it would be used only to pump drinking water. The superintendent, Tom Chick, announced that work would soon be completed on the log cabin, dining room, and restaurant.[7]

Bob-lo Profiles: A Park Is Born

In June 1898, a short six months after the first announcement of the lease, the Detroit News-Tribune *printed a five-page article that reads as though written by a Ferry Company promoter:*

> *There is a common human failing to exaggerate all new enterprises and to try to gloss over shortcomings. However, those who visit the Bois Blanc park are sure to say that it surpasses their expectations. . . . Just where the dock is built are three fine hickory groves. . . . The groves have been carefully trimmed to give an unobstructed view of*

the river. . . . There is not a low, marshy spot on Bois Blanc and consequently, mosquitoes and other insects are unknown. The hickory groves offer a delightful shade; the songs of wild birds constantly float from the lofty crowns.

Throughout the groves are scattered hundreds of rustic seats, swings for the children and hammock posts for those who wish to rest. A fine young locust hedge separates the southern edge of the woods from the adjoining fields, sheep are resting under the trees or feeding in the meadow.

Stately trees are interspersed about the groves and behind pretty white railings are clumps of hardy annuals in the earliest flower beauty of May. The groves have been carefully cleared and the smoothed and ornamental grass has taken firm root, making a wide continuous lawn, like some fine green carpet.

Many Valuable Improvements

The water pipes which feed the water tanks run out about 250 feet under this wharf, a powerful marine pump supplying the power.

The great pavilion, 78 x 125 feet in size, is situated in the hickory grove. The dancing space will accommodate several hundred couples. . . . [A] broad and convenient stairway leads to the tower from where may be had an unrestricted view of the island, lake and river for at least ten miles. . . .

The base ball grounds are laid out in the height of such construction, and are on lines strictly professional. . . . There is a clear field between the fowl posts and in the fielders' gardens. The diamond has been located partially in the grove on either side, where hundreds of persons can easily see the game without being exposed to the sun.

Log Cabin and Bicycle Track

The bicycle track is one third of a mile around, likewise laid out in the best style. It has been carefully prepared on a spot where there is a slope in the center of a field, so that the sides and turns seem almost natural formations, although, of course, they were not built without great care and skill to insure the right angle. . . . Since the bicycle has become universally used, every crowd at the island will be sure to have its interesting races, and many a hot finish may be expected there this summer.

Another novel feature of Bois Blanc park is a large model of the log cabin of pioneer days, at which refreshments will be sold at low rates. The cabin will be fitted with the usual accoutrements of the pioneer times such as bunches of dried fruits, popcorn and medical *herbs, suspended from the log rafters. The great chimney is made of large boulders and the ridge pole consists of a huge oak tree, with the gnarled roots left remaining in a decidedly picturesque way. . . .*

Another unusual feature will be an artificial rocky island composed of huge granite and limestone rocks taken from the lime kiln crossing and brought to a spot where an island is being gradually accumulated. It will be planted with running vines and water plants and will be transformed into a veritable bower where children may clamber about. . . . The lighthouse is sure to be a point of interest to sightseers. Keeper Hackett has been in attendance for many years, and his father was there before him. . . . The pretty dooryard, the garden, and the wide outbank over the lake lends picturesque beauty to the scene. Not far from the lighthouse is an old Indian burying ground, almost lost to view. The ancient block house, a curious primitive fort is immediately to the rear of the lighthouse. . . . The walls are of immense thickness, composed of oak logs. The lighthouse keeper has plowed up arrow heads and other Indian implements near by, and has added them to his collection of relics of other days.[8]

The island park formally opened on June 20, 1898, with a trip by the newsboys of Detroit carried by the *Promise.*[9]

An early newspaper ad featuring the Promise and park attractions. Courtesy Dossin Great Lakes Museum, Detroit, Michigan.

The desire of the shipping companies to maximize use of their vessels led to the creation of new parks as destinations for day excursions. The parks were designed to cater to basic and emerging recreation needs of the time, such as picnicking, playing baseball, and dancing, and company heads like Bielman and Campbell recognized that transportation to and from the parks could not be taken for granted in the quest to lure the greatest number of people to these venues. The next level of competition involved transportation itself. Not only did the companies need to transport the maximum number of passengers from Detroit docks to the parks as quickly as possible so that they could enjoy their time at the park, but they also needed to consider how the mode of transportation could be structured to enhance the overall experience for the customer.

The ships that were now in use to transport passengers to the parks had been designed for different purposes. Either they were constructed as conveyances for short hops across the Detroit River, like those of the Ferry Company, or they were designed for longer runs to other towns such as Port Huron to the north or the cities of Lake Erie. In either case, the primary emphasis was to get the passengers to the destination and, although the creature comforts were provided for the longer runs, little consideration was given to entertainment for the new breed of passengers on their one-day holidays.

Thus, although Campbell may not have been surprised, he was probably dismayed to open the paper one December morning in 1899 to read the headline "Magnificent Fast *Tashmoo* Launched Yesterday." This was the announcement of Campbell's nemesis Bielman that the White Star Line would bring out the first three-hundred-foot passenger steamer for its runs from Detroit to Port Huron with stops at Tashmoo Park on Harsens Island. Frank Kirby, one of the most prominent marine architects of the day and designer of the Hudson River day liners, designed the *Tashmoo* with both the present and future in mind, to accommodate the transit customers going to Port Huron as well as the crowds clamoring for a day at Tashmoo or the newly popular moonlight trips to Lake St. Clair. From the day of her launch that December afternoon, the *Tashmoo*'s sleek profile, two great funnels, and sleek whiteness proclaimed that it would no longer be business as usual on the river.[10]

But Campbell the businessman curbed his competitive nature and refrained from immediately responding in kind to the challenge of the *Tashmoo*. He recognized his first priority as being to the park itself. Having proven Bois Blanc to be a destination success in 1898, his next step was to cement the Ferry Company's hold on the island. In 1899,

while the *Tashmoo* was being completed, he purchased the leased twenty-five acres and an additional seventy acres on the southern half of the island. This enabled him to have in place by the start of the 1900 season a beautiful 250-seat riverside cafeteria designed by Detroit architect John Scott to complement the dance hall and other attractions already in place. The Ferry Company steamers *Pleasure* and *Promise,* designed for the high-volume Belle Isle trade, were easily able to accommodate demand for the park from Detroit. The round trip from Detroit cost thirty-five cents and included music by Zickel's Orchestra. The large steamers were joined by the Amherstburg ferry *Scotia* in delivering customers to the park.[11]

The new cafeteria proved a hit and effectively counteracted the success of the maiden season of the *Tashmoo*. By the 1901 season, the increasing popularity of Bois Blanc was evidenced by its first crowd-related problem, as a headline in the *Amherstburg Echo* announced, "St. Andrews Picnic: Trouble on the Docks":

Hundreds of Scotchmen living in the vicinity of Amherstburg were disappointed yesterday in not being able to attend the picnic of the Detroit St. Andrews Society at Bois Blanc island. A crowd which swelled to over 2,000 people at the Amherstburg dock waited for hours hoping to secure transportation to the island. The Detroit, Belle Isle and Windsor Ferry Company, it is said, refused to carry people across the river and the only means of transportation was the little steamer *Scotia* which could accommodate about 30 each trip. Among the waiting Scotchmen were members of the Malden Council who have threatened to raise assessment fees of the island next year.[12]

But Campbell, accustomed to political threats, shrugged them off and led the Ferry Company in pursuit of its goal: on November 22, 1901, the *Echo* announced the company's acquisition of the remaining 115 acres of Bois Blanc from the Atkinson estate. Except the lighthouse,

Cafeteria interior. Photograph courtesy Dossin Great Lakes Museum, Detroit, Michigan.

the Randall property, and a few small parcels, the island property was now secured, and Campbell could finally swing into action. Within a week he announced that Frank Kirby had been commissioned to design a new steamer for the Ferry Company.

On July 7 the following summer, the *Detroit News-Tribune* headlined, "She's the Pride of the River":

> The *Columbia* made her first public trip on a Monday evening when St. Andrews Society of Detroit held its moonlight excursion on her. The new ship measured 216 feet over all with a 45 foot beam and a draft of 13 feet nine inches. While her government carrying capacity was listed at 3,200 persons, it was report-

ed that she would be capable of carrying "over 4,000 souls" and have a speed of 16 miles an hour or better. Reporters gushed about the new ship's beautiful appointments including the men's and women's cabins paneled and trimmed in mahogany with decorated ceilings. The ship also boasted a dance floor on its promenade deck that was 40 feet wide by 140 feet in length and engines visible from a viewing area on the main deck. On her return trip from Bois Blanc, she made the distance in one hour and twenty minutes including two check downs for bad weather.[13]

Within a few weeks of her maiden voyage, the *Columbia* was beginning to stake her claim to the river. A banner in the *Detroit Free Press* read, "Red Hot Race Down the River: *Columbia* Beats the *Kirby*":

The steamer *Frank E. Kirby* waited yesterday morning and got what she had been looking for ever since the new steamer *Columbia* has been placed on the Bois Blanc route. The two boats were stimulated with all the ginger in their makeup and the race which resulted is described by those who saw it as second only to the memorable speed test between the *Tashmoo* and *City of Erie* June 4, 1901.

In yesterday's affair, as in all the races of this kind, there are two stories as to how it occurred. Those aboard the *Columbia* say she was taken unawares; that she had 100 tons of water in her ballast tanks, the trim tanks were partially full and the shelter cloths were down; in fact, that they had no idea there was to be a race until they saw the *Kirby* swing out from her dock and take after them.

By the time the word was passed to the engineers and the cloth rolled up, the *Kirby* and *Columbia* were neck and neck. All the way to Amherstburg, it was nip and tuck, but when the ships checked down for the Lime Kiln crossing, the *Kirby*, claiming she had to check early for an upbound steamer, was 200 feet behind. One passenger exclaimed "The run from Mamajuda to Ballard's reef was one of the prettiest ever seen in these parts. The wave of white water pushed by both ships was a sight to behold." The running time of the *Columbia* to Amherstburg in this race was fifty minutes. Her scheduled running time was given as an hour and ten minutes.[14]

And so as the steamboat wars heated up, the seeds of the twentieth-century phrase "Getting there is half the fun" took root. The parks that

The Columbia as depicted in an early ad. Courtesy Dossin Great Lakes Museum, Detroit, Michigan.

Have you ever spent a day at

Bois Blanc Park?

Have you had a ride on the big

"Columbia"?

If not, now is your chance. The large excursions for the season are over, the people who have been out of town all summer will be given a chance to visit the most beautiful spot in this vicinity. September weather is always the finest and the Park looks its best. Rain or shine, you can always have an enjoyable day at **Bois Blanc.** There is ample shelter and perfect protection. No liquor, no improper conduct. Every convenience for women and children. Modern Cafe. Popular prices. The best of music. The **"Columbia"** is the latest and finest production in excursion steamboats, and for speed, safety, elegance, and carrying capacity, has no equal. The full orchestra continues until the end of the season.

"Take a Day Off and Be Happy."

The best **Moonlight Excursions** ever given, every **Tuesday** and **Friday** evenings, during September.

All Trips,
    Adults,   35c.
    Children, 25c.

Detroit, Belle Isle & Windsor Ferry Company

dotted the rivers and lakes, including Cedar Point, Put-in-Bay, Tashmoo, Sugar Island, and Bois Blanc, had been created as destinations for a new type of vacationer. Now it was up to the ships to ensure that these customers could enjoy their one-day holidays from the moment they strode over the gangway to the moment they returned to the city.

BOB-LO the Island of Beauty *and* Joy!

1926

Ready for a Good Time

Down the Chute

Come On! The Water's Fine!

Fun and Exercise

The Bob-Lo Light-house that guides all ships to the Detroit River

Landing at Bob-Lo Island

Off for a Pony Ride

More Fun for the Kiddies

The Old Log Cabin

100-Year-old Block House, around which many battles were fought

Bob-Lo Island, or in French, Bois Blanc Island, is situated eighteen miles from Detroit, at the mouth of the Detroit River. It contains 225 acres of shady groves.

This popular Island was named Bois Blanc Island—meaning "white wood"—by French voyagers about 200 years ago, because of the dense growth of these trees.

For twelve years Bob-Lo Island was the property of the United States; but in 1826 United States and Canadian boundaries were definitely outlined, and Bob-Lo Island became a Canadian possession. And so it stands today.

Bob-Lo Island has been the scene of many bitter battles in which the Canadians, Americans and the Indians were the chief participants. It also sheltered many slaves who were escaping from bondage in the South to freedom in Canada.

In 1901, Bob-Lo Island was purchased by the Detroit and Windsor Ferry Company, and made into one of the finest and most complete picnic grounds in the country.

To this Island of rich beauty and healthful recreation, thousands of pleasure seekers travel every day. An atmosphere of gaiety surrounds the Bates Street Dock (Detroit) where steamers leave four times daily.

After an hour's restful sail down the Detroit River, you arrive at beautiful Bob-Lo Island Park—an island whose great picnic grounds, bathing beach, baseball diamonds and beautiful new serve-self cafeteria have placed it among America's leading pleasure grounds. Bob-Lo's Baseball Diamonds are recognized as some of the finest in America.

The cool, refreshing lake breezes that blow constantly over Bob-Lo fill you with a spirit of happiness and self-satisfaction. You are ready to delight in the many amusements offered at Bob-Lo Island Park. You can swim, dance or frolic around on the immense picnic grounds—and after that—lunch!

More healthful, happy recreation—and you are ready for the comfortable, restful sail back to Detroit. Steamers leave Bob-Lo four times daily for Detroit, the last steamer leaving at 8 p. m.

Children's Paradise

Bob-Lo Island has long been recognized as the ideal playground for the kiddies. Its immense picnic grounds, with chutes, swings, merry-go-rounds, pony rides and other joyful, safe amusements have helped to make "Bob-Lo" a household name.

STEAMERS·LEAVE·FOOT·of·BATES·STREET ~   ~DAILY·AT 9·a.m. 10·a.m. 1:30 p.m. and 3·p.m.

DWFC

Dancing on the boats . . . The carousel and power . . . Dancing in the courtroom
. . . Development of the park . . . Bois Blanc or Bob-lo? . . . The sailors monument
and the dance hall

While band music had been a regular feature of river ferries for decades, public dancing was just coming into vogue at the turn of the twentieth century. In the competition to provide a total experience for the customer, the Detroit, Belle Isle, and Windsor Ferry Company's *Columbia* had something the White Star Line's *Tashmoo* did not—a dedicated hardwood dance floor on the promenade deck. The *Tashmoo*'s side-wheel simply took up too much deck space to allow for that luxury. Over the course of the ship's lifetime, dancing space was created in three separate areas, which attests to the difficulties in planning for a multiuse vessel. The White Star ships were designed for longer runs and rolling stops at river towns for which the side-wheel was considered state of the art. The propeller-driven ships were considered optimal design for the cross-river boats of the Ferry Company. Charles Bielman's decision to go with the side-wheel cost him space for a showcase dance floor, and, while the *Tashmoo* was considered the most photogenic on the river, the lack of a dedicated dance space hindered its attractiveness to dancers and especially groups of moonlighters—another relatively new market.[1]

The first and most elaborate construction of the Ferry Company at Bois Blanc in 1898 was a dance casino to cater to the throngs of customers wishing to try the latest steps. But the Puritanical Walter Campbell, determined to manage Bois Blanc with his characteristic iron fist and intent on keeping the park as a destination for the more genteel and family-oriented set, put into place policies designed to keep rowdier elements away. He chose not to install the popular electric lights that had dazzled millions at the recent exposition in Chicago and at Coney Island's Luna Park because he did not want the park to become a "resort for midnight owls."[2] As for the issue of alcohol, Fred Mason, the excursion agent for Bois Blanc flatly declared, "We have no barroom nor will liquor be sold, so our patrons will be exempt from the presence of intoxicated persons."[3] And even though Bois

Blanc Park was born when the ballroom waltz was being dethroned by a wave of newly devised dances that reflected the faster pace of the machine age, Campbell showed himself to be no dancing fool. Having successfully designed the *Columbia* and the island park for dancing, he now took steps to rein in the rowdies. A week before the *Columbia*'s maiden voyage, a headline read, "Stopped New Dance: Ping Pong Tabooed by Ferry Company." The dance in question was described as "more of a muscular achievement than a ping pong game. A couple clinch, affect a tense expression and then go hopping back and forth with short, springy steps . . . attempting to imitate a ping pong ball as it bounces across the floor." The story interviewed a Professor Dufy, a dance teacher, who stated, "It is not a dance; it is a nuisance—a meaningless movement capable of nothing but inconveniencing other dancers." He claimed it originated on Bois Blanc on Decoration Day. Professor Dufy went on to state that he would not allow any "freak" dances in his academy and that "Detroit is given to freak dances to a greater degree than any other city in the country."[4]

With the unseemly elements in check, Campbell set about his task of making Bois Blanc *the* excursion destination for both Detroiters and Canadians. In 1904 a larger steamer, the *Papoose,* was brought into service for the Amherstburg crowds. In 1905 construction began for a huge new two-story building of cut stone and dimensions of 150 x 90 feet to house a carousel to be built by Coney Island's M. C. Ilions and

The Papoose *conveyed passengers from Amherstburg to the island until 1940. Photograph courtesy Dossin Great Lakes Museum, Detroit, Michigan.*

The amusement building was originally constructed to house the carousel. Photograph courtesy Parks Canada Agency, Fort Malden National Historic Site of Canada.

Photograph courtesy Dossin Great Lakes Museum, Detroit, Michigan.

Sons featuring "wooden chariots and hand-carved animals that lope and gallop." The steam organ for the carousel arrived from Germany in time for the 1906 season.[5] To provide electricity to the horses and the lights of the ride, a powerhouse was built. Around the same time, the company launched the new steamer *Brittania*. Although designed primarily for the Belle Isle service and significantly smaller than the *Columbia,* the *Brittania* made several runs to Bois Blanc, the first on July 4, 1906.[6]

The powerhouse was installed to provide electricity to the carousel. It remained in operation as the sole source of power to the island until the 1950s. Photograph courtesy Dossin Great Lakes Museum, Detroit, Michigan.

But dancing, both on and off the boat, still proved the main attraction for most of Bois Blanc's customers, and Campbell and his staff had to do some fancy stepping to maintain the park's reputation as a carefree family destination. During the 1905 season, Samuel Meisner, a passenger on the *Columbia* moonlight, interceded on behalf of another passenger who was ordered off the dance floor for attempting to do a dance "known to coloured people as 'the rag.'" As a result of his belligerence in defending the dancer, Meisner was declared persona non grata and not allowed to cross the gangplank as he tried to board the *Columbia* the following year. Meisner brought two charges against the Ferry Company: the first for humiliation and annoyance suffered when he was unable to meet with "the lady of his choice" at Bois Blanc and the second addressing whether the company, as a common carrier, had the right to refuse passage to anyone.[7]

While the Meisner case made its way through the courts, the steamboat destination wars heated up for Campbell on two fronts: at the same time that the Detroit City Council temporarily halted the Ferry Company's lucrative Belle Isle trade pending the resolution of a fare dispute, the White Star Line purchased Sugar Island (located just one nautical mile from Bois Blanc) and began to develop it as an excursion destination, primarily to expand its Toledo, Ohio, trade. Threatened by the potential loss of Belle Isle and the erosion of the Bois Blanc trade, Campbell began looking for another destination site. He found one closer to home than he had imagined, and in 1907 the purchase of Peche Island, from the estate of Hiram Walker, was announced to the board. Peche Island, located at the confluence of Lake St. Clair and the Detroit River, just off the eastern end of Belle Isle, was smaller than Bois Blanc but large enough for a destination park. Campbell was content to simply hold onto his acquisition as insurance against an unknown future. His only statement on possible development of the island was that it would "cater to the more desirable element of pleasure seekers."[8]

By 1908 a decision had been rendered in the case of *Samuel Meisner vs. The Detroit, Belle Isle, and Windsor Ferry Company*. A lower court concluded, in substance, that the company was not a public carrier in its operation of its line to Bois Blanc Island and could not be forced to transport persons it considered objectionable. The court maintained that the company's line between Windsor and Detroit and Belle Isle might be considered a public carrier but that the Bois Blanc run to the island owned by the company was not. The court awarded Meisner the seventy cents he paid for tickets plus one dollar interest, significantly less than the five hundred dollars he originally sued for. Meisner car-

ried the case to the Michigan Supreme Court. At that level, the Ferry Company argued in its defense that it "caters to a particular class of people. It desires to keep out those whom, for reasons of its own, it deems objectionable. Unless it did this, it would not secure the class of patrons it desires. If it secures the better class of people, which its managers probably believe would make the enterprise a success, beneficial financially to themselves and attractive to respectable people, it must exclude the rough, boisterous, and rowdyish element from its boats and grounds." The Michigan Supreme Court supported the lower court verdict stating that Bois Blanc was considered a private pleasure ground and that the company could exercise any terms of admission it chose.[9] Vindicated by this decision, Campbell continued to exercise control over dancers, as indicated by his statement to the press: "Want to know why we allow dancing on the morning boats to Bois Blanc and not the afternoon boats, do they? Well, it's this way. A lot of people go to Bois Blanc who don't like to dance, don't believe in dancing, and don't like to see it. We permit on the morning boat down and on the evening boat back, but on the afternoon trip we figure it is only right that those who don't care for it should have a chance to enjoy themselves in their own way. That's the plan we have run the excursions on for several seasons."[10]

Improvements to Bois Blanc in 1908 included a new souvenir building, a horse barn, four picnic shelters, and two baseball diamonds. The season ended with the beginning of a new tradition as the townspeople of Amherstburg came down to the riverfront to give a rousing farewell to the *Columbia* upon the final departure from the island dock: "The steamer was loaded with Amherstburg natives for the last trip with the rest of the town's residents standing on the docks giving an ongoing Chautauqua salute. The band of the *Columbia* was on the upper deck and played 'God Save the King' while Captain Wilkins pulled the steam whistle in the pilot house in continuous salute until the boilers were almost out of steam."[11]

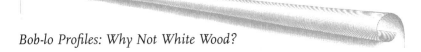

Bob-lo Profiles: Why Not White Wood?

Off the dance floor, there were some things that Campbell was not able to dictate. Many nonfrancophone immigrants, unfamiliar with the proper pronunciation of "Bois Blanc," the name bestowed on the island by the French coureurs de bois some two hundred years prior, took to calling the island "Boys Blank," rendering the island's name meaningless and dispelling its heritage. In 1908 an unidentified utility infielder for the Detroit Tigers was credited with Americanizing the name of the island to Bob Lo, thereby alienating the purists and widening the debate in the press. In an editorial titled "Why Not White Wood?" the Detroit Journal *opined:*

> *By what shall we know the isle of picnic and pleasure which, decorative and coveted as a gold tooth in a past generation, stands sentinel at the river's mouth? Shall we preserve the name and traditions of early voyagers and cling to "Bois Blanc," or shall we immortalize the name and mooted genius by an ex-utility man of the Detroit infield and call it Bob Lo? The deck hands of the ferry boats make a strong*

case for the latter. It's imposing heavy official responsibilities upon a Hibernian sailor to force him to twine his tongue about a rhetorical and historical land mark like "Bois Blanc" while heaving bow lines and shoving gang planks. The name is classic, chaste, ornate dignified and all that. But is it serviceable? Isn't it confusing to behold those impressive letters inscribed upon the sign of the promenade deck and then hear the peanut vendor pronounce it "Boy Blank"?

On the other hand, the Daughters of the American Revolution, rushing to the defense of local history and geographical nomenclature as we knew they would, advance telling arguments against this concession to cowardice—on the part of the officers and deckhands—and linguistic laziness. "Bois Blanc" means something, though some of us have forgotten it. It is pronounced "Bwaa Blaw" and means simply "White Wood." The early French navigators, emerging from the lake or sailing down the Detroit River, saw a little white grove set on an island and, having run short of kings, queens and chateaux in Paris with which to designate the topography, they seized upon the inspiration of the initial impression and did rather well with it. "Bob Lo" means nothing save unappreciated advertising for a baseball player who wasn't good enough to hold his job on the team. With quite as much justice and as little vandalism, we could change Grosse Isle to Gross Zeal. Much more aptly, in view of increasing tendencies toward conviviality, Grosse Pointe would be Gross Pint. Should we phonetify Ponchartrain merely because porters and bellhops tussel with it futilely in the long watches of an endless night? The Detroit, Belle Isle and Windsor Ferry Co. is going at progress much too ruthlessly. The daughters are right. "Bob Lo" will never, never do. Better the meaningless, colorless translation "White Wood" than that.[12]

In spite of, or perhaps because of, the stubborn resistance of Campbell, the Daughters of the American Revolution, and the print media, the general public was steadily gaining ground in its effortless grassroots campaign to adopt the name Bob-lo for the island. Although Campbell would continue to refer to the island as Bois Blanc until his death many years later, the media would slowly but surely adapt to the levels of their readers.

At the end of the 1909 season, the *Papoose* was pressed into service to help complete a new islet off the bathing beach, and the electric light plant was being enlarged with another boiler installed. The major project under Campbell's personal supervision was the erection of a monument along the eastern shore facing Amherstburg to honor Great Lakes sailors. A large, old-fashioned anchor made from cypress, salvaged by Campbell from a Civil War–era steam barge, the *City of Cleveland,* was mounted atop the eight-foot-high structure. One hundred feet of the anchor's chain were draped around the base of the monument. Iron chocks, with the chain running through one of them, were built into the sides of the monument to resemble the anchor's appearance when aboard a ship. Campbell took a modern patent anchor from the *Columbia* and fastened it to the west side of the monument to link the past to the future. The monument's plaque read: "Erected as a tribute to the sailors of the Great Lakes."[13]

In 1910 the Ferry Company launched the *Columbia*'s new running mate, the *Ste. Claire,* thus beginning eight decades of dedicated service by the two steamers to Bob-lo Island. Combined, the vessels gave the Ferry Company the potential to accommodate a much larger clientele to their island than either White Star or Ashley-Dustin ships could handle. The island's proximity to Detroit also meant that the ships could easily manage two round trips a day, whereas the greater distances to Tashmoo Park and Put-in-Bay meant the competition could only make a single trip per day.

In that same year of 1910 the Ferry Company dissolved and reincorporated as the Detroit and Windsor Ferry Company. While the company continued to service Belle Isle, the ongoing feud with the city over the lease rights to the Belle Isle dock had taken its toll. Also likely playing a role in the decision was the continuing erosion of clientele because of the inroads that the Detroit United Railways had made over the years.

The Sailor's Monument.
Photograph courtesy C. B. Wigle.

In the 1911 annual report to the Ferry Company board, Campbell stated:

> The boats of the company are in first class shape. . . . Most of the company's docks are in good repair with the exception of the ferry dock at Windsor and slight repairs at Amherstburg and Bois Blanc. The new bath house was completed in the summer and was much used. The island is in fair shape.
>
> The improvements at Bois Blanc have been in the nature of stone work, riprapping and stone walls and several grandstands for ball fields, repairing roofs and lawn furniture.
>
> I expect to receive this spring from Cuba several palms of all varieties, the cost to us will be just for the freight. In time the plants will be very valuable and will make for decorations for our buildings and grounds on both Bois Blanc and Peche Island.
>
> I am glad to report only a few slight injuries and no deaths. All of which is respectfully submitted.[14]

Reeling from the encroachments first of White Star and then of the Ferry Company, the Ashley-Dustin Line finally responded in 1911 with the launch of the beautiful *Put-in-Bay* for its Detroit run to the Lake Erie islands. Ashley-Dustin now had a ship to run opposite the *Frank E. Kirby* on its Detroit to Sandusky route. The *Put-in-Bay* was more of a liner and sported an enclosed hardwood dance floor on its second deck and day cabins on its third, offering protection from the considerable open-lake portion of its run. Although it had lost a river destination when Sugar Island went to White Star, Ashley-Dustin compensated by adding Cedar Point to its route. The gleaming new ship and added excursion destination allowed Ashley-Dustin to remain in the thick of competition in the still-expanding market.

Never one to stand pat, Campbell revealed his next major move in discussions with his board. The board entertained presentations by two Detroit architects, Albert Kahn and John Scott, for a new building on the island. By January 1912 the board approved Scott to enter into contracts for the materials necessary to build a new dance pavilion. The new structure was to be of steel and stone construction, making it completely fireproof, and, at thirty-five thousand square feet, it would be four times the size of the current dance hall. Iron and steel were to be provided by McClintock-Marshall of Pennsylvania, and the masonry was to be done by Geering Brothers of Detroit.[15] A month later, the *Amherstburg Echo* reported that construction would start as soon as the navigation season opened. Stone would come from the Amher-

The dance hall.
Photograph courtesy C. B. Wigle.

"The smooth, polished dance floor will be a revelation to you." Photograph courtesy Walter P. Reuther Library, Wayne State University, Detroit, Michigan.

stburg quarry so that the exterior would be in keeping with the other buildings on the island, and the new organ would come from M. Colte Brothers in New York City. By the end of the summer a mighty framework of steel rose far above trees in the center of the island.[16]

The dance pavilion was not the only major construction in the area. Just a few hundred yards west of the island, the U.S. Army Corps of Engineers formally opened the Livingstone Channel in October 1912. The Ferry Company steamer *Britannia,* carrying several hundred prominent Detroiters, was the second in a long parade of ships passing through the twelve-mile-long channel for the first time.[17]

On Bois Blanc itself, the former Randall property on the northern end was acquired by Williams Menzies, who in 1912 announced plans to develop a summer hotel with cafeteria and cottages called Point Bob-lo. The hotel was actually a modification of Randall's Lookout Cottage. Menzies ferried passengers to the resort from his own boat livery in Amherstburg and held a grand opening on July 23 with a banquet for sixty guests. But by the next spring, with nothing else built, he had sold the land to Windsor, Ontario, interests and sold all the furniture and bedding at auction. Lookout Cottage became a silent sentinel at the north end of the island.[18]

The dance hall was completed in June 1913, and the local press reported that the high ceilings kept the dance floor cool and comfortable in comparison to its poorly ventilated predecessor, where overheated dancers were a problem. Campbell proudly proclaimed, "Even on the hottest days during the summer the building will be cool and dry." Campbell went a few steps further when he announced that he would not allow any "freak" dancing on the floor. To enforce this rule, he placed an "officer in charge responsible to immediately stop any turkey trots, bunny hugs, and bear dances and to restrict dancers to the regulation two-step and waltz, with exception made for the society walk." While the new pavilion had a gallery overlooking the dance floor, to which the public was admitted free, dancers were charged five cents per couple. The abolition of free dancing represented a decision by the company to recapture construction costs by adopting a policy it

The lavatories were designed to complement the dance hall. Photograph in author's collection.

maintained was much in use at dance pavilions throughout the country.[19]

With the dance hall and customs in place, Campbell turned his attention to some necessary details. He again engaged Scott to design a lavatory of stone to complement the beauty of the dance hall. He also set about acquiring seventy-six acres of water lots from the Canadian government around Bois Blanc, "making our island secure from intruders and encroachment."[20]

It is safe to say that Detroit songwriter Frank Stodgell had Campbell in mind when he penned the tongue-in-cheek final lines to his tune "Bob-lo Song" in 1913:

> Then Home Sweet Home from old Bob-lo
> In the evening when the sun is low
> It's a beautiful ride by the light of the moon
> Dancing home to a rag time tune.

With the addition of the dance hall, Bob-lo came into its own as a destination for Detroiters and Canadians alike. The popularity of the hall and the bands on the boats made endless dancing a Bob-lo reality.

Bob-lo flowers as an amusement park . . . The Whip . . . War, Prohibition, and the Roaring Twenties . . . The dodgems and the Bug . . . The Depression and shutdown . . . Happy New Year . . . The demise of the Ferry Company

Bob-lo had proven itself successful, but Campbell was already thinking ahead. In 1913, although reticent about details, he provided a glimpse into future plans for the development of Peche Island. His ideas included a dining pavilion, a dance hall, and bathing beaches. He said, "It is understood that the park is being designed to cater to the more desirable element of pleasure seekers, and the buildings and amusements will be in keeping with the idea."[1] For the moment, however, Campbell was content to reside with his family in the only building on the island, the former Walker mansion.

The Ferry Company continued to invest in development of Bob-lo. Campbell's 1916 annual report read in part, "We are raising and growing in our nurseries on Bois Blanc and Isle of Peche about 1000 or more trees: oak, ash, maple, elm, walnut, hawthorne . . . and shrubbery for the two islands. . . . The real estate owned by the company has been well kept up and is in fairly good condition. The rigid rules of the US and Canadian governments now make us keep our marine property to the highest point. The boats were examined by Special US Government officials from Washington without exception last fall and pronounced perfect."[2] The annual report also noted construction near the powerhouse of a second stone lavatory, also constructed by John Scott and Company, complete with septic tanks. Now dancers had matching restrooms to both the north and south of the pavilion.

In the summer of 1917, the park complemented the carousel by adding a second ride. The Whip took riders around an elongated flat oval track in little buggy seats. At the curves, the cables attaching the cars to a centrally tethered rail expanded out, accelerating the speed of the cars and whipping the passengers into the back of the seats. It was a variation on the skating game of Crack the Whip played without need of skates, ice, or a rink. The new ride was located immediately off the dock and sheltered in a building made of wood that was not designed to compete with the elaborate stone structure housing the carousel.

The company minutes gave testimony to the ride's popularity, report-ing, "It was a great success and paid for itself in one season."[3]

A couple of years later, Campbell attributed an increase in ferry rid-ership on the river crossing "largely to the fact that they have in Wind-sor a commodity called 'near beer' for sale."[4] Campbell had stuck to his policy of no alcohol aboard his vessels or at his park and now had an act of the U.S. government—the Volstead Act—to support him. Prohibition was now the law of the land in the United States, and the production and consumption of alcoholic beverages was banned. Ca-nadian laws, however, still permitted the brewing of alcohol, beer, and wine, and the Crown government was not as zealous as its U.S. coun-terpart in monitoring consumption. Once on Bob-lo, thirsty Detroiters could travel to Amherstburg to explore the attractions of that town, including its saloons. It became part of the Bob-lo experience for a certain class of adult park goers to hop the *Papoose* to Amherstburg for a pint or two of the famous 4.4 beer and get back to the park before the wife and kids noticed.

For the year 1919, Campbell reported attendance at Bois Blanc to be 316,000 and listed receipts as follows:

Boat Fares	$155,000
Papoose	$5,150
Check Rooms	$6,320
Merry-Go-Round	$12,950
Souvenir Store	$11,000
Dancing	$13,516
Whip	$16,166

Not included were receipts from the cafeteria, Log Cabin, and other commissary operations.[5]

An International Joint Commission study conducted in 1918 definitively linked ongoing outbreaks of cholera and typhoid to sewage contaminated water in the Detroit River. Downriver communities, where the highest bacterial concentrations were found, were at last forced to address the issue of their untreated water intake systems. In his report of 1920, Campbell announced, "We are now compelled to build a complete filtration plant which will assure good, pure water. The Health Commission will not allow us to use the river water without proper process of purification."[6]

The water filtration plant is where the Vernors was mixed. Photograph in author's collection.

For the 1921 season on Bob-lo, the Ferry Company added a couple of shelters for picnickers and a new building at the bathhouse. Attendance was listed at 373,585—down 56,000 from 1920, the first year to break the 400,000 mark.[7] In his 1922 annual report, Campbell compared the Bois Blanc attendance of 391,000 to the 501,000 passengers who rode the Belle Isle ferries, pointing out that the Belle Isle figures were for one-way trips while Bois Blanc's were for round trips.[8]

That report was to be Campbell's last to the Ferry Company board. He died the following summer at his home on Peche Island. The *Border Cities Star* wrote in Campbell's obituary, "Always did he have his work at heart, and for years, Mr. Campbell made it a point to be at the foot of Bates St., Detroit, at 9 o'clock in the morning and at 3 o'clock in the afternoon, to order the start of the boat to Bob-lo Island."[9] The *Detroit News* obituary for Campbell related:

> Through the years he was in charge of the Detroit and Windsor Ferry Company, Mr. Campbell was totally devoted to his task and he could be found almost daily on the wharves where his boats docked. He was especially concerned for the comfort and safety of his passengers, especially the women and children, and for this reason his boats were always temperance boats. No liquor was ever permitted on his ferries or Bois Blanc boats nor would he permit Sunday dancing on the trips to the islands.[10]

Walter Campbell's death coincided with the end of another Ferry Company institution, the operation of steamers to Belle Isle. Since 1879 Ferry Company boats conveyed thousands of Detroiters from the downtown docks to the city's recreation gem, but with the completion of a new bridge, the automobile finally won the day. On the night of November 28, 1923, the Detroit ferry docks burned, forcing the Ferry Company to temporarily shift service to the Joseph Campau docks of the Walkerville Ferry Company.

The new president of the Ferry Company, Ralph Gilchrist, was far less outspoken than his predecessor, as evidenced by his barebones reports to the board and little media coverage. Records from his era of leadership indicate only receipts and disbursements punctuated by passionless announcements. His reports on the 1923 season provide only a financial statement for Bob-lo, with receipts totaling $295,000 against disbursements of $105,000. By comparison, receipts from the Belle Isle ferries were only $63,800. The new ferry building at the foot of Woodward Avenue was listed as costing $183,000.[11]

Subsequent annual reports from Gilchrist indicate other revolutions and trends at which Campbell would have balked. For example, Campbell might have perceived as invasive to his island kingdom the modern technology of an underwater phone line that was laid in 1924 to connect the island with the mainland. And although revenues from the dance pavilion rose from $13,500 in 1920 to a healthy $35,900 in 1925, this increase was due in part to the lifting of some of the restrictions previously placed on the dancers.[12] People in that lively era were going to find places to do the Charleston, and Bob-lo had plenty of competition. Since revenues from the pavilion were on the upswing, it was only good business to go with the times.

While the twenties were good for business at amusement parks, the new roads and interurban streetcars that now connected cities had cut deeply into the primary Detroit-Toledo route of the White Star Line. The company, in reorganization, discontinued that run and its stop at its Sugar Island Park near Bob-lo. The *Tashmoo* would now run to Port Huron, and the Sugar Island rides were moved to Tashmoo Park on Harsens Island. While White Star ships would still use Sugar Island and its dance hall as a moonlight destination, Bob-lo became the only downriver amusement park.[13]

A report from the Ferry Company's attorney to the board in February 1925 summarized the property holdings on the island. Although the Ferry Company completed purchase of John Atkinson's acreage by 1901, there were still parcels of land on the island they did not own. The summary stated:

> The properties owned by D&W on Bois Blanc Island at this time include 205 acres of high land and 76.5 acres surrounding the island. These were purchased accordingly:
>
> 1899—South part purchased from Atkinson for $21,500
> 1901—North part purchased from Atkinson for $20,000
> 1913—Water lots purchased from Province of Ontario for $3,825

The Company owns the entire island except four land parcels and two water parcels:

> Parcel 1—The Randall property (also known as Menzies or Stone property), 3.8 acres
> Parcel 2—Water lot in front of Randall property
> Parcel 3—Lighthouse property, 2 acres

Parcel 4—Water lot in front of lighthouse

Parcel 5—The Keena property on W. side of island (deeded from Atkinson to Keena, 1889), 343 feet of river frontage by 300 feet deep

Parcel 6—The Wilkins property (also known as Wardell property) next to Keenas, 100 feet frontage by 300 feet deep, deeded from Keena to Wardell, 1889.

As mentioned earlier, the British Crown had acquired Bois Blanc from First Nations tribes (Ottawa and Chippewa) and then sold the island to Colonel Arthur Rankin. The Ferry Company's attorney reported that the patent to Bois Blanc Island granted to Arthur Rankin was never registered and that he was having it registered as well as having certificates of taxes issued for the various properties. The issue of ownership was thus addressed and not raised again until the end of the twentieth century.

A more dramatic legal issue with immediate ramifications occurred just before the island officially opened for the 1925 season, when the Ferry Company issued this statement through its Canadian attorney: "The Detroit and Windsor Ferry Company has been advised through the local immigration inspector in charge at Windsor, acting on advice

A 1926 map of the island. Courtesy Dossin Great Lakes Museum, Detroit, Michigan.

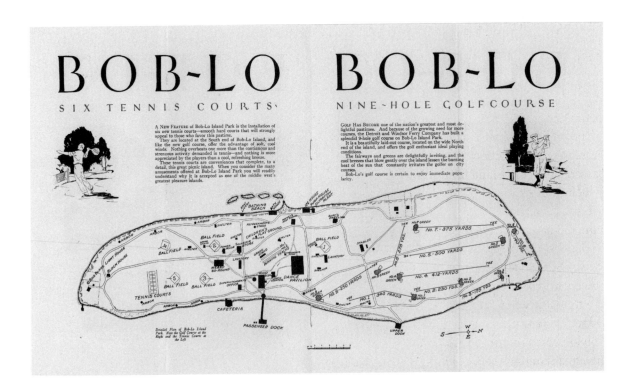

from Ottawa, that passengers going from Amherstburg to Bois Blanc Island on the steamer *Papoose* are not to be subjected to United States immigration inspection. Therefore, the steamer *Papoose* will not carry passengers to the island from Amherstburg until this is ironed out."[14]

Before this time, it had been customary for U.S. immigration officers to be stationed on Bois Blanc and question passengers coming from Canada on the *Papoose*. Their purpose was to prevent immigrants from using the *Papoose* as the first leg of a journey to the United States by way of the *Ste. Claire* or *Columbia*. By allowing U.S. immigration officers to screen the *Papoose* passengers at the island dock a handful at a time, the Ferry Company did not have to subject its thousands of Detroit passengers to immigration questioning on their return from Bob-lo, which was in Canadian territory. The Ferry Company's decision to discontinue service was greeted with dismay:

Storm of Protest Expected from Amherstburg as Result

A storm of protest is expected from Amherstburg where merchants and others have done a considerable trade with Americans who visited the mainland who arrived at the island from Detroit. The situation, in this regard, is particularly acute in connection with the sale of 4.4 beer, as a large trade in this beverage had been looked forward to this summer.

Although Bois Blanc is part of the province of Ontario and a large restaurant is operated there, the ferry company which owns practically the whole of the island, will not take out a beer license. There have been rumors that a restaurant with a beer license, might be erected on a small piece of island territory not owned by the company, but this is now considered unlikely for the reason that the ferry people would strenuously oppose any such proceeding and would undoubtedly take steps to keep its patrons from making use of such liquid facilities.[15]

The impasse was resolved when Canadian customs officers set up shop on the island dock and deliberately went through each and every picnic basket brought onto the island by passengers from Detroit. The resulting four-hour backup onto the island caused the company to reconsider its decision, and service from Amherstburg was restored, much to the relief of all involved. The inspection of passengers returning to Detroit was reduced to manageable proportions by stationing U.S. immigration officials on the island dock to conduct a cursory inspection of the crowds as they boarded the return boats.

In May 1925 the *Amherstburg Echo* cheerily reported, "A new Vernors ginger ale factory has been installed on the west side of the island and a Vernors stand was set up in the dance pavilion at the same time."[16] Soon after, a baseball diamond on the north end of the island was converted to a nine-hole golf course, which opened on July 3, 1926.[17] Attendance was just above four hundred thousand for both 1926 and 1927. The name "Bob-lo" appeared in the company minutes for the first time in 1927, and a brochure proclaimed "Bob-lo Island: Where Fun Begins." Bob-lo stayed out of the news and company minutes for the next couple years but reemerged with an announcement in the *Echo:* "Stone Building Built to House Little Auto Coasters."[18] The dodgems had arrived.

While Bob-lo continued to thrive, there were reports upriver that the amusement parks along Jefferson Avenue at the foot of the new Belle Isle Bridge were being condemned. Coupled with the era of auto

(Opposite page)
Aerial views of the island ca. 1930.
Photographs courtesy Dossin Great Lakes Museum, Detroit, Michigan.

Cartoon ads from the late 1920s. Courtesy Dossin Great Lakes Museum, Detroit, Michigan.

Courtesy Dossin Great Lakes Museum, Detroit, Michigan.

ownership and the still-expanding street railway system, the closing of the Jefferson Avenue parks paved the way for the new suburban amusement parks Edgewater, Eastwood, and Jefferson Beach, none of which were accessible by water. The street railway system was following the model that the steamship companies established decades earlier by creating destination sites of their own. These new parks would compete with Bob-lo for the next fifty years.

The Ferry Company's operating statement for the 1929 season indicated the Bob-lo boats netted the company over ninety-two thousand dollars, representing almost a quarter of the company's net profit for the year. On the island, a partial breakout of revenues by percentage showed that the commissary and souvenir revenues significantly outperformed the amusements.

The ledgers through the 1920s indicated that operating expenses and revenues for the Bob-lo boats were running very close. It was important for the company to get people to the island so that they could spend money. The management saw the boat ride, amusements, and dancing as attractions to the island but hoped the need for refreshment between amusements would generate spending on items that produced the greatest profit margin, food and souvenirs.[19]

Then, the November 29, 1929, edition of the *Amherstburg Echo* announced, "New Amusement for Bob-lo: D&W Ferry Co. Has Force of Men Installing the Bug":

TABLE 1. 1929 ISLAND REVENUES (DOES NOT INCLUDE PURCHASES MADE ON BOB-LO STEAMERS)

Amusements		Commissary	
Dodgems	6.66%	Log Cabin	21.27%
The Whip	6.48%	Cafeteria	20.07%
Aeroplanes	5.90%	Souvenirs	8.42%
Bathhouse	4.82%	Whip stand	7.00%
Merry-go-round	4.73%	Soda fountain	3.07
Dancing	3.78%	Playground	2.35%
Golf course	1.34%	Check room	1.26%
Putting green	0.76%	Merry-go-round stand	0.94%
Boathouse	0.40%	Dance stand	0.75%
Total amusements revenue	34.87%	Total commissary revenue	65.13%

"The Detroit and Windsor Ferry Company is embarking on one of the most ambitious projects in their history this fall and next spring," Ferry Company General Manager Capt. Fred Simpson announced. "I have just come from Bob-lo with a representative of the company which is installing the Bug Ride, an exciting new amusement which is expected to be one of the most popular on Bob-lo Island."

Simpson went on to describe the two railroad cars of sand and gravel needed for the foundation of the ride which would be located between the Dodgem and the Whip. He described the ride as a "rollicking device which combines all the thrills of a roller coaster with complete safety."

He went on to note that children had not been neglected in their plans as evidenced by a new miniature Ferris Wheel that would adjoin the playground. He was also pleased to announce the new Brownie Coaster which he described as "a railroad train on a slightly undulating track and seemingly propelled by two Brownies pumping a hand car, but which is actually run by electricity." He went on to stress that "this amusement provides open air cars working on the highest safety principles and dimensioned expressly for the youngest folk."

Billboard Magazine, in its review of the 1930 season, announced the addition of the Bug to Bob-lo but noted that the ride was also installed at Eastwood, Jefferson Beach, and Edgewater parks.[20]

While these new rides were going up, the nation's economy was going down, and the Great Depression was under way. Perhaps sym-

The Bug. Photograph courtesy Dossin Great Lakes Museum, Detroit, Michigan.

bolic of this downturn, the island lost two pieces of its past. First, on January 31, 1930, the lighthouse residence burned. Although the lighthouse had been automated in 1927 and there was no longer need for an onsite keeper, the residence was tied to the development of the island from the past century. Island descriptions written more than twenty years after the fire noted that it was still possible to see the outline of the Hackett family's garden between the lighthouse and the blockhouse. The second loss occurred on the last day of the 1931 season. The *Amherstburg Echo* headlined, "Old Randall Mansion on Bois Blanc Island Totally Destroyed in Daylight Fire." The story related a grass fire that engulfed the Victorian mansion known as Lookout Cottage, which had been built in 1888 by James Randall.[21]

Prohibition wars made their mark on the Bob-lo operation in a couple of different ways during this period. The first was during the winter when the river froze over to allow liquor-laden trucks to travel directly from Amherstburg across Bob-lo to Grosse Ile and the U.S. mainland. The second was during the summer when a passenger on the *Ste. Claire* was wounded in the crossfire between the border patrol and rumrunners transporting a cargo of liquor from Canada to the United States. This latter event contributed to the growing anti-Prohibition sentiment that argued that the public was paying too high a price for enforcement of a failed social experiment.[22]

Revenues declined precipitously from 1930 to 1932, when the Bob-lo operation was unable to show a profit for the first time and the park was open only seventy-two days.[23] The *Amherstburg Echo* announced that "due to economic conditions, excursions and moonlight rides to Bob-lo will be discontinued for the first time in 35 years. . . . The *Ste.*

The Bob-lo police force.
Photograph courtesy Marilyn Robertson.

The Aeroplane Ride. Photograph courtesy Walter P. Reuther Library, Wayne State University, Detroit, Michigan.

Claire and *Columbia* will remain at their docks in Windsor and the island park will not open this year."[24] The 1933 Ferry Company annual report tersely announced, "The Chair . . . made a fact that Bob-lo had not been operated during 1933—operation considered unwise due to economic conditions . . . 1934 operations dependent on conditions picking up."[25] But while the Ferry Company was forced to curtail services, one of their competitors, O.J. Dustin, manager of the Ashley-Dustin Line, announced that activities of his lines would increase in 1933 and that the steamer *Put-In-Bay* would travel to Cedar Point, St. Clair Flats, and Put-In-Bay.[26]

Of course, the revenue downturn was not the only concern confronting the Ferry Company board. In 1929 the new Ambassador Bridge opened to traffic, followed a year later by the first cars to flow through the Detroit-Windsor Tunnel. This one-two punch caused the Ferry Company to draw up a statement of planned obsolescence for the U.S. Internal Revenue Service to document the loss of their business caused directly by the new competition. America's unabated romance with the motorcar was in full flower, and people found it more convenient to go with the flow. The advent of bussing from downtown Detroit to downtown Windsor was more appealing to pedestrians who previously had no alternative but to throng the decks of the cross-river ferries in all types of weather. This, combined with the Depression, sent the Ferry Company onto the ropes and placed all their operations, including Bob-lo, in jeopardy.

It did not take long for would-be predators to sense the weakness of the beleaguered Ferry Company and begin to move in. After the second full season of closure, the *Amherstburg Echo* announced, "New Pleasure Resort North End of Bob-lo: Company Headed by Former Local Man":

> With the idea of acquiring the north-eastern portion of Bois Blanc Island and making an amusement park out of it, a new company, the Island Lines Limited, has been formed and granted a Dominion charter. The organization is headed by Captain Orval L. Duncanson.
>
> . . . At the present time, this new company has an option on the land in question, also an option of the Canada Steamship's excursion steamer, the *Rapids Queen,* which they propose to run from Detroit to this new park.[27]

The new company proposed to build a large dance hall out over the water at the northern end of the island, provide hotel accommodation for several hundred guests, include picnic grounds and playgrounds, and have a bathing beach on the eastern side. Ferry service from Amherstburg was part of their scheme. The opening date was set for Decoration Day 1935, with construction work on the buildings scheduled to begin in the spring.

The property in question, the northernmost point of the island, was once owned by James Randall and was where Lookout Cottage had stood. Duncanson had already arranged for several bargeloads of fill from the Livingstone Channel to be dumped off the northern end of the island, demonstrating how creative use of the water lots could expand the island to accommodate the breadth of his proposed undertaking.[28]

Duncanson's action got the attention of the Ferry Company. Three months later, the *Amherstburg Echo* headlined, "Happy New Year for Everyone: Bob-lo Park Will Open Next Year Says Captain Fred J. Simpson":

> Capt. Fred J. Simpson, vice-president and general manager of the Detroit & Windsor Ferry Company, is giving the town of Amherstburg . . . one of the finest New Year's Presents it could possibly receive, when he said, "You may announce in the Echo this week that we intend to open Bob-lo park next year and operate it daily to the highest degree of efficiency as to picnic pleasures and ferry service.

"... It is not news at all to say that the decision of the Company to keep Bob-lo closed the last two years was a sad blow to Amherstburg and heaped trouble on its shoulders additional to the burdens of the depression.

"... Later on, when spring opens, it will be necessary to employ a force of men to clean up the park, make the gardens, carry out a campaign of painting and of putting the whole island in shape ..."

Captain Simpson's announcement calls for three cheers and a tiger.[29]

With this announcement, no more was heard from Orval Duncanson's group.

As the park reopened, the golf course was closed and the carousel building converted to a convention hall with the ride moved to the center of the island.

Riding this wave of optimism and acknowledging the repeal of Prohibition—but not racism—the Ferry Company's annual report given in January 1935 read, "Bob-lo will be operated in 1935 and we have announced new evening service and will prepare island for same. . . . Tickets at 65 cents for day excursion and 75 cents for evening. . . . We are addressing policy of no beer on island or day boats and are considering the question as to evening boats. On question of Mr. Paddock, the Chair stated that only our own boats run to island and maintaining same as a private park helps our patrons to handle the negro problem."[30]

Through almost four decades, the Ferry Company board had waged a battle to keep "undesirable" elements away from the island park. In the city of Detroit, institutional segregation confined blacks to the Black Bottom ghetto near downtown and away from venues designed for whites. But the industrial boom and its promised jobs lured thousands of people to Detroit, and the swelling black population was threatening to burst through the seams of Black Bottom and flood through all walks of Detroit society. From the perspective of the board, the prospect of blacks riding and dancing on the boats and enjoying themselves on the island presented the possibility that their white customers would seek their amusements elsewhere and forsake Bob-lo.

In an attempt to accommodate the black populace, the owners of the Ferry Company, Ashley-Dustin, and White Star followed the compromise example of other amusements and sporting events and offered their facilities on designated "Colored Days." These separate but equal days were usually offered on Mondays, otherwise low revenue days for their operations.[31] Recalling a painful time in his boyhood during the early 1930s, former Detroit mayor Coleman Young remembered, "That summer our class scheduled an eighth grade graduation party at a local amusement park known as Bob-lo, which is still located on an island in the Detroit River. As we were loading the boat to take us to Bob-lo, one of the guides jerked the cap off my head to check out my hair and officiously informed me that black children were not permitted at the park. Despite my Boy Scout experience and all of the things I'd heard from my father and other black adults, I honestly wasn't prepared for that. And I was never quite the same person again. My sister Juanita must have been as taken aback as I was, because to this day she refuses to go to Bob-lo."[32]

Bob-lo did not come all the way back to solvency in 1935. In its eighty-eight days of operation, the park attracted 230,000 patrons and ended up almost fifty thousand dollars in the red. Although more than they had lost in 1932, this was less than they had to spend to maintain the island the previous two years that they did not operate. The golf course was closed and the carousel building converted to a convention hall, with the ride moved to the center of the island. The company authorized a survey for a submarine cable to connect the island to Ontario Hydro to supplement the electricity generated by the powerhouse. Although the survey was completed, the company elected not to incur the expense of laying the cable at this time.[33]

The company decided to send a questionnaire to excursion organizers and received responses from eighty-seven group representatives. They found that a significant number of respondents cited high prices and competition from other companies as having worked against the success of selling tickets for group outings. While two respondents referred to the absence of beer as a deterrent, fifteen responded that the ban on liquor was a primary reason their group members preferred Bob-lo. In response to the question "Would you like to see beer served next year on the boats?" sixty-three answered no, and only twelve answered yes. But by far the greatest number of respondents mentioned two factors as being key to their preference. The first was the clean, respectable, wholesome atmosphere and good supervision, and the second was the boat ride, its distance from the city, and the length of time visitors were able to stay on the island.[34]

While the resuscitated Bob-lo was beginning its second year of renewed operation, something happened that helped secure its future as an amusement park, at least for the time being. On the evening of June 18, 1936, the *Tashmoo* left her dock at Sugar Island full of

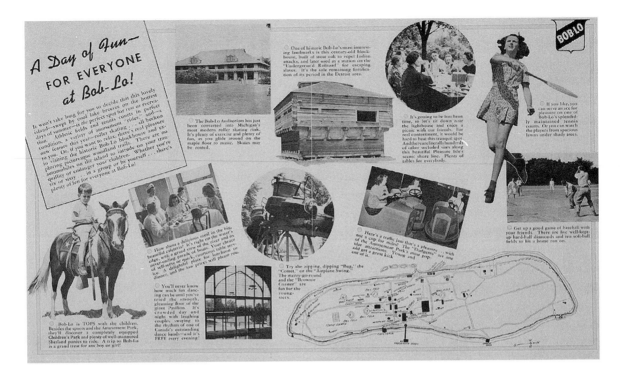

moonlight revelers. Within a mile of the dock, while cutting toward the downbound channel near an area called the "Hole in the Wall," the ship struck a rock in the riverbed tearing a gash in the bottom of the hull. While she successfully made it to a dock in nearby Amherstburg before sinking and without injury to any of her passengers or crew, efforts to raise the ship resulted in a broken keel and the sad end of what many regarded as the sleekest ship to ever run the river.

The end of the *Tashmoo* also signaled the end of Sugar Island as a moonlight competitor, leaving the entire lower river to Bob-lo. While Bob-lo continued to show faint signs of revival, the Ferry Company's annual report was filled with concerns for the future of the company in light of the continued loss of cross-river customs to the bridge and tunnel, and in that year the Ferry Company made its first proposal to sell the cross-river ferry operation to the state of Michigan. But before another annual meeting had taken place, Gilchrist, Campbell's successor, died, leaving the company in dangerous waters without an experienced captain at the helm. With vice president and general manager Fred Simpson too ill to step in, board member Joseph Vance was voted into the chair and, at the annual meeting of January 1937, stated that "the sale of the ferry operation shall not in any way prevent or hinder the operation of the company's excursion business including the operation of the *Columbia* and *Ste. Claire* and the operation of its amusement park business at Bob-lo."[35]

On May 15, 1937, the *Detroit News* reported, "Detroit and Canada Tunnel Corporation to Buy D&W Ferry Co." The article stated that the Ferry Company's Bob-lo boats would continue to operate. Less than a week later, the *Detroit Free Press* ran another earth-shaking headline: "Bob-lo Steamers Get State Beer License."[36] Even with the repeal of Prohibition in place since 1933, the Ferry Company's new president must have sensed the ghost of Walter Campbell hovering nearby. Vance took pains to assure the Michigan Liquor Control Commission that the company was proposing to sell beer only on the night runs. The "temperance" boats would be dry no more.

Campbell's memory may have influenced Vance in other ways. He emulated Campbell by taking a personal interest in the day-to-day Bob-lo operations. One July day he rode the boats to the island and recorded the following observations:

1. Clock at head of main stairway on *Columbia* not running.
2. Our two excursion boats report and clear once a day at Amherstburg, which is under arrangement. Customs at Detroit are not requiring clearance.
3. Our souvenir store is closed on Sunday. Mr. [Charles] Park reports an opportunity for good Sunday sales. Store was closed some years ago on complaint of a Lord's Day Alliance of Toronto. Stores at Niagara Falls are open Sundays selling souvenirs. Amherstburg stores are open Sundays selling ice cream and souvenirs. Superintendent Park recommends putting in ice cream and ginger ale in souvenir store and keeping same open on Sundays.
4. There is no mirror in men's lavatory in café which looks unusual.
5. Mr. Park wants water at south end of island for users of ball diamonds.
6. The "No Smoking" sign in black cabin on *Columbia* should be removed. Saw high class old lady being flagged for smoking (and on a pleasure boat!). Sign looks as if it were made about thirty years ago.[37]

With canned beer successfully introduced on the boats, Vance issued a memo with specific suggestions to determine costs for the following:

1. Public address system for use on the dance floors of the ships
2. Means for broadcasting returns of baseball games to the island
3. Equipment necessary for dispensing draft beer in evenings on first deck and deck above the dance floors
4. Changing motors or replacing Dodgem equipment to permit bumping.[38]

The memo also raised the issue of the cost of Finzel's Orchestra on the boats and wondered if college orchestras could be investigated for that purpose, although that risked the "danger of creating trouble among the boat crew for their non-union character." He asked his general manager, Captain Simpson, to explore the Detroit and Cleveland Navigation Company and Georgian Bay Lines to see if they had looked into this, but the gravely ill Simpson passed away before this could be investigated.

Vance sent another memo in early 1938 to his Bob-lo management team, including Superintendent Park, to implement the changes for the coming season and to purchase a new ride, the Flying Scooter (Comet). Regarding music on Sundays, he asked for responses to Park Engineer Courtney's suggestions for the following:

1. Dance Pavilion Organ—suggests this be put in condition by Wurlitzer if we can get him on island. Thinks Grinnel's representative is no longer in Windsor, and last time he was on island he short circuited the organ so that only one half of it operates. We do not need any new rolls for organ.
2. Whip Organ—Suggests we purchase three boxes of music.
3. Merry Go Round organ—Suggests we purchase two boxes of music.

The Whip and Merry Go Round music should, of course, be different. The German make is much better and it should be ordered now if we are to have it before the season opens. He suggests that we purchase standard rather than modern music.[39]

Courtney's suggestions for improvements also included recommendations for the addition of ponies, enhancement of the lawns, and the addition of trees and flowers to the park. He also proposed a shelter to protect the merry-go-round (an indication that it had been left unsheltered since removal from its original building the year before), a redesign of the dodgems, and new streamlined cars for the Whip.[40]

Photograph courtesy Dossin Great Lakes Museum, Detroit, Michigan.

UNDER NEW
MANAGEMENT
1938–1949

Transition of ownership . . . Managed by Georgian Bay Lines . . . The girl in the roller rink . . . War again . . . Living on the island . . . "Colored Days" and the Sugar Island solution . . . The Supreme Court finds Bob-lo guilty . . . An unhappy fiftieth anniversary

As the 1938 season was getting under way, the Ferry Company received notice that the U.S. Department of Commerce had approved its acquisition by the Tunnel Corporation. The Tunnel group, whose only real interest was in eliminating the competition, bought out the Ferry Company's cross-river operation rights while leaving them the rest of their assets, including the steamers and Bob-lo and Peche islands. The last cross-river ferry ran on July 18, 1938.[1] At a special meeting held a month later, the former Ferry Company board voted to organize a new corporation to be named Bob-lo Steamers Incorporated and focused its attention solely on the business of Bob-lo. Joseph Vance continued his role as president, and Harry Fletcher was elected the new company's vice president.[2]

During the 1938 season 273,000 passengers sailed to Bob-lo from Detroit, with an additional 19,500 traveling to the island by way of Amherstburg, numbers well below those of the peak seasons of the 1920s, when attendance topped 400,000. To somewhat compensate, a change from canned beer to the draft variety increased beer revenues on the boats by 30 percent. Beer outsold Vernors and all other soft drinks, which had the advantage of being sold on both boats and the island, combined. After the season, the ferry *Papoose* was retired from service on the Amherstburg run and replaced by the *Kawandag II*. The 1939 rates were announced with Tuesday through Saturday boat fares at seventy-five cents reduced to fifty cents for Sunday and Monday. The board also approved a plan to offer special seventy-five-cent dinners at the cafeteria.

Perhaps feeling that they had nothing to lose, the board voted to request that both Peche Island and Bob-lo be ceded by Canada to the United States. With the Union Jack replaced by the Stars and Stripes, the new company would be freed of the vexing immigration-related issues that had resulted in the threats and slowdowns that had affected attendance on several occasions. With another war looming, the board of directors had only to review old advertisements from World War I to see the warnings prohibiting U.S. males of draft age from coming to Bob-lo without a special permit.[3] While the request had little chance for success, the board felt it needed to do something to get both governments to help rather than hinder their efforts to get people to Bob-lo. The board also voted to petition the Canadian government to allow Sunday souvenir sales on Bob-lo, arguing that other Canadian attractions were allowed to do so.[4]

At the first meeting of 1939, Vice President Fletcher moved to engage the services of William B. Mayo and his company, the Chicago, Duluth, and Georgian Bay Transit Company (popularly known as the Georgian Bay Line), to manage Bob-lo for the season.[5] The motion to outsource management of the Bob-lo operation, a major departure from past practice, was passed. Although they were concerned that management of Bob-lo Steamers Incorporated would take up much of their time, the board of the Georgian Bay Line voted unanimously to enter into the contract.[6] Within two weeks, the Georgian Bay Line announced to the press that they would take over management of Bob-lo and that the *Columbia* and *Ste. Claire* would be equipped with oil burners. They also announced that their overnight passenger ships The *North American* and the *South American* would use the old Ferry Company docks at the foot of Woodward Avenue.[7]

Mayo, president of the Georgian Bay Line, and his board wasted little time in further exercising their duties. They installed seven electrical refrigerators on the island and on the boats and upgraded the Vernors plant. Besides converting the engines from coal to oil, they streamlined the ships' smokestacks and repainted them in Georgian Bay Line colors. They sold the Amherstburg vessel *Papoose* and brought electricity to the Woodward docks to provide shore power to the ships. On the island, they introduced pony rides and roller skating, the latter in the building once occupied by the carousel. Mayo even proposed bringing the Detroit Symphony Orchestra to the island for concerts. In another sign of changing times, Mayo declared that the bathing beach be closed because of pollution. Although the water filtration plant now provided safe drinking water to the island, the mix of industrial effluent and lack of sewage treatment in upriver communities had finally taken their toll on the water quality of the river.[8]

In June the *Detroit Free Press* ran two Bob-lo–related articles. The first, a standard promotional piece, reported, "Bob-lo Steamers Start 41st Season." The article announced that iceless refrigeration for drinking fountains and cafeterias had been installed. It also mentioned a special Sunday scenic trip to Port Huron.[9] The second article was not for promotional purposes:

Bob-lo Invaded, 4 Net $10,000

Detroit and Canadian police were searching for 4 armed bandits who invaded Bob-lo by speedboat and robbed the resort of receipts of $10,000. The four each carrying a sawed-off shotgun landed on the north end of the island. . . . One of them slugged the night watchman, knocking him unconscious. They then herded two cafeteria employees into offices where they smashed the company's fire steel safes. They were heard to leave the island at 4:00 A.M.[10]

Another blow to the Bob-lo economy was felt as fewer companies elected to treat their employees and their families to a picnic on the island. Although unions took over sponsorship of these events, one Bob-lo official lamented, "Union-sponsored picnics do not make up

Courtesy Dossin Great Lakes Museum, Detroit, Michigan.

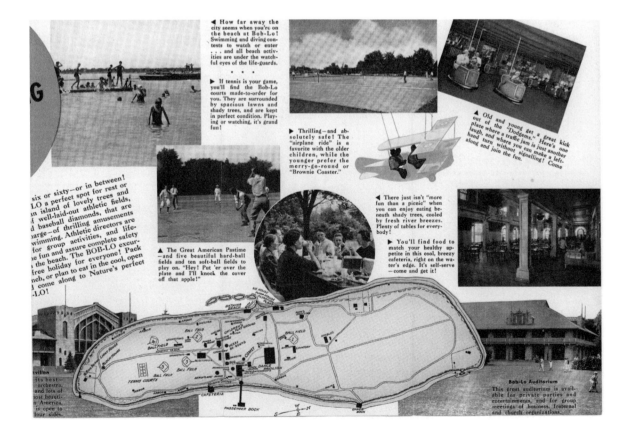

for loss of company-sponsored picnics."[11] Yet, even with the robbery and the loss of company events, in July *Billboard Magazine* reported, "Bob-lo Does Best in a Decade."[12] The Chicago, Duluth, and Georgian Bay Transit Company reflected this good news in their annual report: "The Bob-lo operation proved very profitable netting our company $17,835 for management services."[13]

In February 1940 *Billboard Magazine* announced that a new corporation—Bob-lo Excursion Company—had taken over Bob-lo Steamers Incorporated. Harry Fletcher, vice president of the former company was named president of the new company, a Michigan corporation with a capitalization of $513,000.[14] Besides Bob-lo Island, its buildings, and the boats, this figure included the Detroit docks, buildings, and property of the old Ferry Company, including Peche Island and the ferry ships *Cadillac, LaSalle,* and *Brittania* (the laid-up ships each valued at $1).[15]

The May 1940 minutes of the Georgian Bay Line noted that the Bob-lo Excursion Company was unwilling to renew the 1939 management contract. The Georgian Bay Line board proposed a new contract with the Bob-lo Company that would pay them one thousand dollars a month for the entire year for management services. Fletcher let it be known he would prefer to negotiate directly for the services of Mayo and not the company, though he ultimately agreed to the Georgian Bay Line proposal for the year.[16]

The *Amherstburg Echo* announced a kink in the works early in the 1940 season with the cessation of the ferry service from Amherstburg to the island for security reasons related to the impending war. The paper referred back to a similar scenario in 1925 that was resolved with the introduction of U.S. customs officers on the island to ensure that immigrants could not use the Amherstburg–Bob-lo–Detroit route as a means of illegally entering the United States. However, in this case, with the world situation appearing increasingly dire with the rise of Nazism, there was no immediate solution to the problem, and Canadians other than Bob-lo employees wishing to travel to the island were forced to get there on the big boats by way of Detroit. Exceptions were made every year with three "Canadian Days," when boats ran only from Windsor and Amherstburg to the island, thus avoiding the need for customs. The *Papoose*'s replacement, *Kawandag II,* a very pretty mahogany boat considered poorly designed for passenger use, was retired to the shores of the island.[17] By the end of the season, however, *Billboard Magazine* reported, "Bob-lo Island Is Up 10% Despite Handicapped Start." In spite of the border restrictions, all departments of the park shared in the increase, with the new roller rink proving a particularly good draw.[18]

Bob-lo Profiles: The Girl at the Roller Rink

Virginia Barclay worked on the island from 1935 to 1945:

> At fourteen, I was the youngest employee hired on Bob-lo. They normally hired college-aged kids. They needed people then, and my aunt was the boss at the Whip Stand, a confectionary stand located between the Whip and the Bug. We sold pop, ice cream, and popcorn. Mr. Park was the park superintendent. Mr. Johnson was responsible for the commissary. I met my husband to be on Bob-lo at the Log Cabin in 1937. He lived on the island with his brother and sister-in-law. They got the island ready every spring. During the winter, my husband and his brother would take his daughter, Marilyn, across the ice to school.
>
> I worked in the Whip Stand until the day the roller rink opened in 1940 in what was the old merry-go-round building. In 1935 they moved the merry-go-round to the center of the island. The large stone building became a hall where we would serve banquets for conventions and the like until they decided to put the roller rink in there.
>
> On the first day of the 1940 season, Mr. Johnson came to me and said, "Virginia, how would you like to work in the confectionary stand in the roller rink?" He whispered it because that was where everyone wanted to work.
>
> Harry Dubey made the ginger ale. They'd get ice from the river in the winter and store it in the barn near the water plant. They'd chop the ice for the ginger ale in the summer. They'd mix the syrup right into the tanks, add the carbon dioxide gas, rock it back and forth a few times, and bring it to us to serve. It was awfully good. We served orange and Vernors, that was it. We used real butter for the popcorn.
>
> The following year, 1941, they started to hire kids from Amherstburg to work the rink floor, and it was part of my job to train them. Mr. Johnson didn't want me to leave the confectionary stand, but Mr. Park wanted me to work the rink. Mr. Mayo (company manager) was elderly, and he'd come over with the Fletchers—the new owners of Bob-lo—to look at the island. I remember he would put on skates and I would hold his arm and skate around with him. Eventually,

I became the pro at the roller rink. I patrolled the floor, skated with people without partners or preparing for competitions, helped with cash, took tickets, just about everything except work the rental room.

I worked in the roller rink until 1945. We worked from the eleven o'clock morning boat to eleven at night. On some nights the boat couldn't handle all the people going back to Detroit, so it would have to take a load at eleven and then the other boat would be called from Detroit to get the rest. That meant we would stay open at least another hour until that boat could get here. There were some nights when the island was so crowded that the eleven o'clock would have to drop its passengers and come all the way back to the island to get the rest that the second boat couldn't handle. Then we were really open late. Those people probably didn't get back to Detroit until almost four o'clock.

From its very first year, the roller rink was one of the most popular places on the island. People would line up for tickets from the rink all the way back to the lavatory. Clubs from Detroit would book their picnics. They'd clear the floor, and they would put on a demonstration show. When the rink was first opened and drawing huge crowds, they talked about converting the dance hall to a roller rink and had me go over there and skate while they tested the floor for load bearing. They didn't think it would work so decided to keep everything where it was. On my breaks, I'd go over there and listen to the music.

When anyone on the island was hurt or took ill, we'd take them over to the Women's Cottage. Mrs. Foster was there to take care of people. We had quite a few broken arms at the roller rink. I remember a sailor who tried to stop himself by throwing his arms out to the rail and his arms just buckled—compound fracture. So when the doctor came over there, he said to me, "Virginia, take hold of his hand and when I say, 'pull,' you pull." This kid had no anesthetic—nothing—and I just pulled and the doctor ironed his arm out, put him in a splint, and got him on the boat back to Detroit.

I was paid $3.50 a day for that job—it was a lot more than many of the others on the island. I think I was the highest paid girl there. I had a lot of extras too. When the cafeteria was still over the river, the chef would send over a hot meal for me. People loved to come to Bob-lo just to sit and dine and enjoy the view up and down the river.

On weekend evenings, I'd take a break and watch the couples coming off the boat to go to the dance hall. The women would wear formal dresses, and a lot of men wore evening wear. But then there were the guys from Hamtramck who would come over wearing their Zoot suits with the chains hanging down and those wide brimmed fedoras. Just a gang of guys. Sometimes they'd have riots there and the police would throw them into that fenced enclosure on the first deck of the boat for the ride back.

Just south of the roller rink were the ponies and bicycles for rent. There was just a bike trail—no racing track at that time. That's where all the Scottish picnics were held. There were baseball diamonds too. We had employee teams called the Log Cabin Spiders and the Cafeteria Rats and would play before the island opened. Sometimes we'd go for a swim and they might bring ice cream over to where we were.

Mr. Courtney was the engineer responsible for the powerhouse on the island. He would row over there every morning to make sure there was power up for the day. It was a steam-powered operation, and when new workers came on the island, it was customary to send them over there for "a bucket of steam."

I took the Maudie *over to work every day with Captain Sanders. When it was really stormy, a smaller boat called the* Rook *would be called over from McQueen's to take us because it could handle the waves.*

In my work era, blacks had mostly custodial or dishwashing jobs. I remember one of the workers came over to the roller rink to watch and Mr. Park accused me of encouraging her to be some place she wasn't supposed to be. Max Simpson, who was black, lived on the island all year round and when one of his family wanted to communicate with him, they'd have to come to the shoreline and he'd come down to the river bank and wave to let them know he was okay. He'd work on the truck that went around the island doing general maintenance and every once in a while they'd stop and watch us skate. They were one of the most respected families in Amherstburg.

When I went back there in the 1980s, the roller rink had been closed and they had converted the building into some kind of show hall.[19]

In early 1941, the Georgian Bay Line board met with Fletcher to renew the contract and to explore the possibility of obtaining office space in the Bob-lo building at the foot of Bates Street. But Fletcher was not interested in continuing the relationship with the company, preferring to engage Mayo and Hatch independently. When the Georgian Bay Line board demurred, talks broke off and the two companies ceased their arrangement.[20]

War-related problems continued to haunt the Fletcher operation. One of the first Canadian Days in 1941 turned out badly, as over

The roller rink in full stride.
Photograph courtesy Bob Barclay.

three thousand women and children from a Sunday school outing were stranded on the island until the early morning hours, victims of overcrowding. While company officials blamed the church planners for overselling the event, the churches contended that the company should have been able to accommodate the crowd.[21]

The incident highlighted a growing problem with the success of Bob-lo. While the unique transportation system set Bob-lo apart from all other amusement parks and the ninety-minute ride downriver was recognized as one of the park's greatest assets, the capacity of the boats was a limiting factor. With the park attracting holiday and weekend crowds exceeding ten thousand, getting enough people off the island to avoid overcrowding of the last boat became a challenge. There was nothing to force people to take the early boat back at four o'clock, or even six, which created overcrowding situations for the later boats, especially on beautiful full summer days when daylight lingered until well after nine o'clock. There were many nights when a "double back" boat had to be dispatched from Detroit when it became apparent that the last scheduled boat from the island was forced to depart leaving hundreds of angry customers still on the island dock. Island staff were asked to keep attractions open to entertain the people until the rescue boat, at least ninety minutes distant, could get there, creating long nights for workers. Another problem was created by couples who would intentionally miss the last boat back, preferring to spend the night frolicking in the groves beyond the dance hall and roller rink. Management finally erected fences that stretched the width of the island to keep those areas off limits.

As the United States entered the war and Detroit went into overdrive to supply the arsenal, Bob-lo and other amusement park managers faced new types of problems. Having sufficient labor for the parks was an issue, as many U.S. and Canadian citizens answered the call to the draft or to work in the defense industries. The labor shortage and the rising union movement combined to give the advantage in disputes to employees. On Bob-lo, park employees were upset that their paychecks were routinely overdue. In protest, an impromptu strike was called one morning just before the park opened for the day. The management in Detroit was alerted and sent the checks to the island by car to beat the boat and end the walkout before the first customers crossed the gangplank onto the island.[22]

The war also affected the boat crews, who, as merchant mariners, could be enlisted to work on ships involved in the war effort. Prior to the 1943 season, the Bob-lo owners announced that the decision to open was dependent upon the U.S. government allocating crew sufficient to operate the vessels. The owners stated that they were also reliant upon the Canadian government to allocate sufficient coal to operate the island's powerhouse.[23]

With plants beginning to run around the clock and women entering the work force, families and young people were challenged simply to find the free time to travel to amusement parks. However, Canadian and U.S. families rose to the challenge to demonstrate that they could both work and play hard. With fuel approved for the Bob-lo boats but severely rationed for personal autos, annual attendance at Bob-lo almost doubled to well over five hundred thousand for the war years even though there was no ferry service from Amherstburg to the island. In 1942 the thirty-five-hundred-passenger steamer *Theodore Roosevelt* was employed by the company to provide midweek transportation to the island from Toledo and Cleveland (a five-hour trip each way) and to handle expanded moonlight and charter business as well as a Sunday cruise to Lake Huron.[24]

Courtesy Dossin Great Lakes Museum, Detroit, Michigan.

The demands of the factory schedules meant that Sunday became the busiest day on Bob-lo and that the 8:45 PM boat was the second most popular time to go to the island during the week. Island employees working the dance hall often had to call the island security force to break up fights between groups of Zoot-suiters from Hamtramck and Detroit who came to let off some steam from the hard work week. The dance hall served over one hundred thousand customers annually over this period, running neck and neck with the dodgems but behind the Bug in popularity.[25]

Bob-lo Profiles: Living on the Island

Marilyn Robertson was born in 1934 in Amherstburg:

> *My dad was working on the Livingstone Channel, and it iced over and he couldn't get home for three days to see me in the maternity home.*
>
> *We lived on the island for three years, from 1941 to 1943. My father was the off-season manager of the island—nine months out of the*

year. During the summer he was chief of the Bob-lo police force. He had seven men under him.

We lived in the house that had been the McKee Rankin house. That house was gorgeous. It had eight bedrooms and marble fireplaces and a grand staircase. One corner of the house was one of the old block-houses that it was built around. There were beautiful furnishings and carpets. Chests with marble tops that were cold to sit on. There was a caretaker's house and two big barns nearby. Mr. Oakes, who man-aged the pony rides, and his wife lived in the caretaker's house, and they housed their ponies in one of the barns during the summer.

When the island was open I had the run of the park. Went on all of the rides, got to eat wherever I wanted, had my choice of horses to ride. In the off season, I was free to go from end to end and covered that place. I liked going to the lighthouse with my dad. The one day I wasn't allowed to roam the island was the day of the Shriner's picnic. They would come off the dock with a snake wrapped around their necks. And they got rowdy too. My dad hated snakes and wouldn't let me near them on that day.

There were a couple of cottages further north of us, but the people were only there for the summer. The other side of the fenced-off area was where the horses could graze. It was fenced off because of the private property but also because there was a sewage lagoon and they didn't want anyone playing around there. The island had no other sewage treatment at that time. If it didn't get to the lagoon, it drained right into the river.

The only problem with living in that house was that they shut down the hydro power and filtration plant over the winter months. We didn't have power or drinking water. So we had to shut a lot of the house off to keep it warm. Four full bathrooms, but we couldn't use them after September. I still have a coal oil lamp that we used for light back then. We had a huge pile of firewood outside in the fall.

When it got cold and the river froze over, I crossed a path they laid out on the ice to go to school on the mainland. Cliff Thompson made the trail and drove stakes into the ice, and they'd check it every morn-ing. They had a boat with runners on it, and if the ice was a little iffy, they made me climb in the boat. Otherwise I walked behind it so long as I held on to the boat. The rest of the time I rode the Maudie *back and forth. One time we got caught in a storm and couldn't land at the work dock. It blew us down river, and we had to land at the big dock.*

The cafeteria over the river was something to behold. White linen tablecloths, good china, real silverware. Good cooks. It was a high-end place. You couldn't go in without a suit and tie. The island was such a pretty place. Especially on the first day of the season, everything would be freshly painted and the gardens would be in full bloom. The dance hall had wooden rocking chairs situated all around the top floor. A bed of Canna lilies was just outside, and the grass was cut to perfection. The Vernors people would come over and fill the tanks that were right inside the water filtration plant. We'd draw a pitcher every night. You could see the souvenir stand from the roller rink. That was a beautiful building as well.

The main Rankin house burned a few years after we left, and only a little bit of the mansion and the blockhouse was left standing. Rollie Spencer, the ride supervisor, moved into what was left of the house after that. The rest of the blockhouse remained until 1970, when it burned. I worked for two summers on the island as a teenager. It didn't hold the fascination for me that it did as a kid. The old cafeteria was gone, and, later, the beautiful dock was replaced by a sunken ship.[26]

In the summer of 1943 the city of Detroit erupted in a race riot that was initiated by white sailors and blacks on Belle Isle. Although a rumored assault triggered the outbreak, Detroit had been building toward this for decades. In 1916, when Bob-lo was still in its infancy, the black population in Detroit was under 20,000. Thanks first to the assembly line and then to the war, increased job opportunities helped the black population multiply tenfold to over 220,000 by 1943, but because of the segregated housing policies of that era, those people were jammed into the same tiny neighborhoods of Black Bottom. By the time the rioting stopped and the dirt had settled over the caskets of those killed in the mayhem, Detroit would not be the same for people of either race.[27]

Blacks were strongly discouraged from participating in the white social world, which included venues and destinations such as Bob-lo. The Bob-lo Island police were responsible to monitor passengers coming off the boats to ensure that no blacks had slipped onto the boat at the foot of Woodward Avenue. They would arbitrarily eyeball the patrons to determine whether or not their skin color would allow them to pass onto the island. The occasional "Colored Days" advertised by the company were offered as much to build an otherwise slow Monday as to provide equal access to the black community. Black churches and social groups were allowed to charter the boats for moonlight cruises, and this seems to be how most Detroit blacks from that era remember Bob-lo.[28]

On the island itself, blacks from Amherstburg were hired only for specific kinds of work. Women were hired to work in the kitchen of the cafeteria, and men and women were hired as lavatory custodians. A few men would also be employed as seasonal labor in preparing the island in the spring and maintaining the properties over the fall and winter.

Early in 1945, *Billboard Magazine* headlined, "New Sugar Island Park Announced: Detroit Negro Spot Opening." Two Detroit business-

In author's collection.

men had formed a company to revive Sugar Island, which had been dormant for almost a decade since the sinking of the *Tashmoo*. The new owners had contracted to use the former Detroit and Windsor car ferry *Wayne* to serve as transportation to the island. The article concluded, "It is expected that the park will reduce racial friction."[29] The new owners set about lining up potential investors to restore the island and to create what they hoped would become a Bob-lo for black people.

The fact that blacks were effectively prohibited from Bob-lo was emphasized in June of that year, when Sarah Ray, a black woman in the company of twelve white women who were fellow students at the Detroit Ordnance Training School, was evicted from one of the boats by crew members before it left the Detroit dock for Bob-lo on a regular day excursion. Through the NAACP, Ray filed a criminal complaint in Detroit against the Bob-lo Excursion Company. Her attorney argued that Bob-lo was a common carrier and, as a Michigan corporation, was subject to the laws of the state of Michigan. Commenting on the case and Bob-lo's policy of racial discrimination, Joseph Bannigan, Wayne County prosecutor, stated, "The discrimination by the Bob-lo Excursion Company has been the most vicious type imaginable since in many cases it was directed toward children who were simply attempting to enjoy an excursion with their schoolmates or other friends."[30]

In November, Judge John Maher of Recorders Court convicted the company of violating the state civil rights act and fined Bob-lo twenty five dollars. Realizing that this decision would affect their ability to refuse admission to blacks, the company appealed to the Michigan Supreme Court, claiming its operations were "foreign commerce" and therefore not subject to the Michigan civil rights statute.

With the case pending, the Bob-lo Excursion Company managed to stay out of the news for 1946, the only notable island change being the demolition of the original cafeteria restaurant over the river, one of the park's first attractions, its supports now considered unsafe. The cafeteria operation was moved to the less elegant Whip building located near the main dock entrance. The Whip was moved outside and a roof constructed over it.[31]

The beginning of the 1947 season brought both good and bad news. An agreement had been reached between the U.S. and Canadian governments that allowed Canadians to go directly to Bob-lo through Amherstburg for the first time in six years. The company began searching for a vessel for that purpose, having disposed of the *Kawandag II* when it broke its keel while being pulled up on the Bob-lo shore several years earlier. Since 1940, except for the Canadian Days every summer when

(Opposite page)
Courtesy Dossin Great Lakes Museum, Detroit, Michigan.

the *Columbia* and *Ste. Claire* would operate exclusively between Windsor and Bob-lo, Canadians wishing to go to the island were forced to go by way of Detroit. Now they were again able to transit from Amherstburg. This good news was tempered by a threatened strike by the crews of the *Columbia* and *Ste. Claire,* members of the Seafarers International Union who were demanding an increase in pay. A company spokesperson was quoted as saying that the wage demands of the crew were so high they might not be able to open the island at all.[32]

The spokesperson's pessimistic comments could have been affected by the even worse news that came the day before the strike threat: the Michigan Supreme Court upheld the lower court decision that the company was in direct violation of the Michigan civil rights statute and therefore had broken the law. The court held that the excursion vessels were under Michigan regulation as public conveyances and had no legal authority to exclude blacks from its boats.[33] The president of the Detroit NAACP, Rev. R. L. Bradby Jr., stated, "It is hoped that the Bob-lo Excursion Company will accept this decision and attempt to comply with it in the full spirit of the law. To continue their former policy of forcing the evils of discrimination on unsuspecting children would be a great disservice to American principles of justice and fair play."[34]

As the 1947 season got under way, attorneys for Ray filed a lawsuit seeking ten thousand dollars in damages from the company. The company responded with an appeal to the U.S. Supreme Court in the hope that its argument as a carrier in foreign commerce would receive a more favorable review at that level.[35] But a successful 1947 park operation was overshadowed by the February 1948 *Detroit Free Press* headline "Bob-lo Discrimination Ruled Out: Excursion Firm Loses in High Court":

> The Supreme Court by 6 to 2 decision held that the Michigan law forbidding discrimination in public accommodations on grounds of race, color or creed applies to the Bob-lo boat excursions even though they are a foreign commerce.
>
> The Boat Company contended that the State Civil Rights statute did not apply to foreign commerce or to interstate commerce. Justice Wiley B. Rutledge in a majority opinion said "there is no national interest which overrides the interest of Michigan to forbid the type of discrimination practiced here."
>
> Justice William O. Douglas, in a concurring opinion in which Justice Hugo L. Black joined, indicated a state law compelling discrimination might be overruled. But the existing state law

forbidding discrimination, he said, falls within the national pattern of uniformity essential for the movement of vehicles in commerce. Justice Robert Jackson, who with Chief Justice Fred M. Vinson, dissented, said the majority view was based on the idea Bob-lo commerce is not very foreign. Justice Frank Murphy (Michigan) took no part in the case.[36]

Justice Rutledge dismissed the company's foreign commerce defense, stating, "Except for the small fenced-off portion reserved for the lighthouse and three cottage sites, the island is economically and socially, though not politically, an amusement adjunct of the city of Detroit."[37] In rendering its decision, the court reviewed several other actions throughout the country for possible relevance to this situation. The court dismissed the relevance of the 1908 *Meisner v. Ferry Company* suit on the grounds that that complaint was not based on any infringement of the Michigan civil rights statute. In testimony before the court, Bob-lo's assistant general manager stated, "The defendant adopted the policy of excluding so-called 'Zoot-suiters,' the rowdyish, the rough and the boisterous and it also adopted the policy of excluding colored."[38] In an accompanying article headed "Bob-lo Firm to 'Alter Policy,'" Wilson W. Mills, attorney for the firm, stated only, "We have no other choice."

In other news from downriver, the Dunbar and Sullivan Dredging Company, one of the major contractors for Livingstone Channel maintenance, announced that they had purchased Sugar Island from the Detroit owners, who failed in their efforts to establish an amusement park for blacks. The former owners asserted that they were "thwarted in their efforts" and that, besides being denied mainland dock facilities, their own vessel was sunk at the dock and power lines to the island were cut. They reported that there was "constant trouble." Shortly after Dunbar and Sullivan acquired the island "as a gift to the downriver community," the remaining structures were burned under suspicious circumstances. Dunbar and Sullivan later announced plans to develop the island as a residential community.[39]

Bob-lo was again thrust into the limelight on June 18, 1948, when scores of people dressed in turn-of-the-century garb traveled to the island to commemorate the fiftieth anniversary of the park's opening. Among the dignitaries aboard that day were Detroit mayor Eugene Van Antwerp, who had ridden on the first cruise to the island as a newsboy in 1898, and British consul general D. F. H. Brickle. A plaque was unveiled on the anchor monument that read:

Dedicated to the 134 years of friendship across 4,500 miles of unfortified border protected only by the mutual respect and understanding one nation holds for the other. Commemorating the 50th anniversary of the Bob-lo Excursion Company and the 50 years of Canadian–American use of Bob-lo Island as an international recreation center.

Presented in the name of the border cities, Detroit, Windsor and Amherstburg.[40]

On this occasion, Charles E. Park's years of service were recognized when island employees presented him with a diamond ring.[41] Park was one of the first employees hired by the Ferry Company for its new Bois Blanc operation in 1898. He was purser of the *Promise*, the first boat to make the run from Detroit, and had the distinction of taking the first ticket from the first passenger to board the boat. He was also the same Charles Park who, in 1906, demonstrated the Rag to the judge presiding over the Meisner suit. He served as superintendent of the island for many years and was, after fifty years, still a part of the operation as general passenger agent.

Just a month after this happy occasion, on July 31, the International Joint Commission issued results of a study conducted to assess the amount of air and water pollutants discharged by ships. The study found that 84 percent of ships passing Detroit emitted objectionable smoke. From this point forward, the Michigan Bureau of Smoke Abatement would issue citations. In that era, company policy for the steamers was to "Throw everything overboard," including garbage, beer bottles, and anything else, even deck canvas, which was replaced every year.[42] But now, with the effects of pollution visible in air and water, the public was becoming aware of the effects of pollution upon the quality of life. Ships would not be allowed to "blow their flues" through their smokestacks while passing the city and industry, and the cities themselves would now be expected to install sanitary sewers to cut direct discharges of pollutants into the Detroit River.

In the amusement park sphere, change was a continuing motif. The postwar availability of the family car and a ready supply of fuel enabled families to take vacations away from the city. Older parks, like Bob-lo, that had survived the Depression and the war years were now facing a public with more options for their amusement dollars. In 1948 the Hudson River Line dissolved, putting out of operation a 250-acre amusement park and four steamers in the Hudson River. Oliver Dustin, principal owner of the Ashley-Dustin Line and its steamer *Put-in-Bay*, died, leaving that company leaderless.

The Bob-lo Excursion Company's final report for 1948 showed combined Detroit and Amherstburg passengers to Bob-lo at just over four hundred thousand, a significant decline from the war years. The park's reigning venue, the dance hall, showed an even more dramatic decline as parkgoers began to shift their attention to other attractions like the new scootaboat ride.

And then, in late December, Detroiters woke up to the news "Bob-lo Faces End of Long Service: Stockholders Vote to Liquidate." Ralph Fletcher, company treasurer, said the excursion boats would be sold or "otherwise disposed of." He maintained that the decision to liquidate was reached because of increasing labor demands and operating costs. Fletcher said no buyers had been found yet for the excursion line, and, "if none show up the boats will be scrapped."[43] Suddenly, after fifty years, the future of the island park, so recently celebrated, was very much in doubt.

The Browning brothers save the day . . . A captain's daughter . . . The Wild Mouse
. . . The *Canadiana* . . . Boom times . . . The Bug derails . . . The riots . . . A real
roller coaster . . . The *Papoose* Fleet and the *City of Wyandotte* . . . Competition in
changing times . . . Enough

As the new year 1949 dawned, the future of Bob-lo became more un-
certain. In February the Detroit and Cleveland Navigation Company
announced they would operate the *Put-in-Bay* for 1949 and that they
were also interested in the Bob-lo operation. A month later, Windsor
mayor Arthur J. Reaume proposed that the island be purchased by the
Canadian government and turned into a national park.

On May 1, 1949, just as it appeared that Bob-lo would not reopen,
the Browning Steamship Lines announced the purchase of Bob-lo. The
company used capital from their subsidiary Lake Iron Corporation to
purchase the two boats and Detroit docks and property, the equipment
on the island, and the island itself from the Bob-lo Excursion Company. The Brownings paid $549,000, which included everything but
the government lighthouse and private cottage land on Bob-lo.[1] Peche
Island remained with the Fletchers.

The Browning brothers showed that they were ready for the ride.
The company reorganized its management structure for the new ven-

In author's collection.

ture. Troy Browning was president of the Browning Steamship Lines. Lorenzo (Red) Browning was a vice president and responsible for Bob-lo Island operations. Bill Browning was also a vice president and general manager and, because of his Great Lakes shipping experience, responsible for the operation of the ships. Another brother, Ralph Browning, ran the commissary and later oversaw island ride operations before becoming manager of the Bob-lo Detroit docks.

One of the first decisions made was to form two companies—the Bob-lo Company in the United States and the Island of Bob-lo Company in Canada. It was hoped that the latter company would enable the management to bypass U.S. and Michigan law and use the point of island admission as a means to refuse access to "undesirable" patrons.

The date of the sale meant that the Brownings had very little time to prepare the island for the 1949 season. Bill Browning recalls, "The island was in basically good shape when we got it, but it wasn't developed as an amusement park." They maintained Charles Park as a consultant that first year and hired Harold Gorry as park superintendent.[2]

Bob-lo Profiles: Divine Intervention

Noted Detroit historian Frank Woodford celebrated the last minute purchase as a victory for both Bob-lo and the city:

CRUISING DOWN TO BOB-LO
That doughty mariner, Troy Browning, has announced that the excursion boats will be running on schedule this summer from Detroit to Bob-lo Island. And those who feared for Detroit's culture, in the face of a threat that there would be no more trips to the downriver island, may set there minds to worry about other matters.

Detroit would not be Detroit without its Bob-lo and the excursion boats. Among the local citizenry there are two schools of thought on the subject of the trip to the island.

One holds that the real charm and value lies in the boat ride itself—that smooth glide down stream, past the west side waterfront and then, as the channel turns, along the marshy Canadian shores which don't look much different today than when the Indians and French voyageurs paddled their canoes over the same route.

The other school of thought adheres to the principal that the island itself is the real attraction, with its carnival atmosphere of Ferris wheels and roller skating rinks.

In my humble opinion, both of these factions have missed the real point.

Bob-lo's real value to the community is as the traditional Mecca for Sunday school picnickers. It is the true pilgrim's destination.

Every year for the past fifty years, the Sunday school kids and the church excursionists, of every creed and sect, have made Bob-lo their port of call.

Young 'uns who regularly skip church through the winter months and surreptitiously spend their collection nickels at the corner candy store, generally get converted about this time of year, as the time comes for the annual excursion.

They wash their necks a little cleaner on Sunday mornings; they deport themselves a little more properly. They take no chances on missing out on the great event.

Observation over a long period of time leads to the conclusion that Bob-lo and the prospects of a Sunday school outing have done as much to advance the cause of religion and morality in this area as any one other thing.[3]

On June 18 *Billboard Magazine* headlined, "Bob-lo Opening Big" and announced plans for a new miniature train for the island. It was also noted that the SS *Wayne,* the same ex–Ferry Company boat that was intended for use at the ill-fated Sugar Island park only a few years earlier, would run to the island from Toledo.

In September the Bob-lo Company was awarded $382,740 by Recorders Judge Paul Krause for its dock property east of the foot of Woodward. Club Bob-lo, consisting of a bowling alley, bar, and restaurant was included in the property to be taken over for construction of the Civic Center. The company built a new dock west of the site immediately in front of their offices.[4]

Besides their Bob-lo operation, Browning Steamship Lines was involved in several ship-related operations. In 1951 Troy Browning was instrumental in the conversion of three C4 World War Two cargo ships to Great Lakes service. The ships were considered ideal for Great Lakes use because of their size and stern-based engines. Although the ships were actually purchased by Republic Steel, the Browning Lines held the contract to convert and manage the vessels.[5] To assist in the conversion operation, Browning promoted the chief engineer from the *Columbia,* Fred Smitka, to assistant fleet engineer. With the three new ships, the *Tom M. Girdler,* the *Charles White,* and the *Troy Browning,* the

Browning Lines had eleven steamships under their management. The new ships were renowned as among the most handsome and fastest on the lakes, with speeds more than twenty miles per hour, and the *White* was proclaimed the winner in unofficial races with the *Cliffs Victory* for lake supremacy.[6]

In 1953 the Browning Lines purchased the *Put-in-Bay*, out of service since 1951, and proceeded to plunder the unused ship for life jackets and other equipment for their steamers. They sold the rest of the ship for scrap, and it was burned in Lake St. Clair that fall. Before the park officially opened, the company continued a tradition of "shakedown cruises" to invite the media to visit the island and preview new attractions for the year. Troy Browning wanted to add flair to this event and asked his staff to take turns creating a theme for this annual activity. One year it was Hawaiian; the next, Mexican. But after a few years, Browning felt that the reporters abused the hospitality, drinking too much and reporting too little, and the tradition came to an end.[7]

At the time of purchase in 1949, all rides on the island were owned outright by the Island of Bob-lo Company. New rides added to the park in the 1950s and 1960s were often owned by individuals in partnership with the Island of Bob-lo Company. The Round Up was the first new ride added in 1954, bringing the total of rides for teens and adults to fifteen. This was followed the next season by a new Kiddieland, which included the Turnpike, merry-go-round, auto ride, and Comet and, along with the Brownie Coaster and pony rides, gave the park its first concentrated area for little children. A landscaping project included the park's name planted in large floral letters facing the river adjacent the boat dock.

On the boats, the Joe Vitale Orchestras were in place on both ships. The end of the 1955 season marked the retirement of Captain Wilkins of the *Ste. Claire,* who had been with the company since 1900. He was replaced by Captain Yonkers, who continued the tradition of longevity by masters of the *Claire,* as she was known to her crew.[8] Attendance at the island that year increased to its best level since the Browning takeover, topping the six hundred thousand mark for the first time.[9]

With shared ownership, major maintenance of the rides was the responsibility of the outside partners. The Island of Bob-lo Company provided day-to-day maintenance and operators. The proceeds were split sixty-forty between the partners and the company. Many Bob-lo staff invested in the rides. One investor recalled, "We thought we'd get rich through the partnership, but all we did was okay." The games of chance were put in by Fred Silber, who split revenues with the Bob-lo Company. The food operations were company owned. At first, Troy

Browning was a great cook and wanted to serve gourmet food in the cafeteria. Upon discovering that Bob-lo customers really did not care for his upscale recipes, they were replaced by those of the ABC Food Company.[10]

Bob-lo Profiles: A Captain's Daughter

As a young girl in Amherstburg, Elizabeth Thompson, daughter of Cliff Thompson, captain of the Maudie, *took advantage of her father's position to go to Bob-lo as often as possible:*

> *I grew up in Amherstburg and went to school there. But the biggest thing in my life was that I spent a lot of time on the* Maudie *with my dad. My dad, Cliff, had the job as captain of the* Maudie—*the tug that pushed the island work barge—and had to transport everything over to the island. Cliff was born in 1906. He started working there in the 1920s and didn't retire until 1968.*
>
> *The* Maudie *was the work boat and left the Amherstburg dock at 5:30 AM sharp every day. The* C. E. Park *was the passenger ferry, and the park staff would ride it to work. Unless they were late; then they'd have to catch the* Maudie *over there.*
>
> *He would usually work until 4:30, but it wasn't unusual for him to work overtime. He loved to be on the river. He would work the river to the island for as long as the boat could get through the ice. He was part of what was known as the island "Park Gang."*
>
> *The* Maudie *was an old boat. It'd be out in the channel and the engine would conk out, and my dad would have to blow the horn to get the* Park *to come get him. Other times the hold would start flooding and we'd have to get the bilge pump going, and my father would tell me to get down there and start to bail. When the* Aquarama *came through the channel, it would suck all the water away from the shore and the* Maudie *would roll all over the place.*
>
> *The* Maudie *transported everything to the island. That included the Vernors, 7-Up, and Borden's trucks. If those trucks weren't blocked under the wheels, they could roll right off. We almost lost the Borden's truck one day when it slipped the gangplank. Cliff called for everyone on shore, fishermen and everyone, to grab a rope and hold the truck steady so he could get the barge back under it.*
>
> *Cliff brought celebrities over on the* Maudie *too. I remember meeting Sagebrush Shorty, who brought over his horse, a palomino. I got*

to sit on it. One day he brought over Roy Rogers and Trigger, but he had a trailer to stay in that had to be hauled over too because he was a big star.

I had the run of the island, especially in the off-season, and I would run in the woods and play in the blockhouse and around the lighthouse. I played with Troy Browning's grandchildren and Dorothy Tresness's granddaughters. There was a house that we called the Spencer house in the center of the island. Part of it was an old blockhouse. We'd go and catch wild rabbits around there. Rollie Spencer was the ride superintendent. The Spencer house was located near the Women's Cottage, where my mother worked. The upstairs of the Women's Cottage was where the park superintendent, Mr. Gorry, and his wife lived, and she cleaned up those rooms as part of her job.

Although Amherstburg was a segregated town, I don't recall any restrictions on black families from Amherstburg going to Bob-lo. Money was the biggest restriction, and my dad would help get those kids there. For a lot of my friends in Amherstburg, the Maudie was the only way they could afford to take a girl to Bob-lo on a date. Cliff would take them and tell them when he was coming back. I was able to take my friends with me and ride whatever rides I wanted free because all the ride operators knew my dad.

But my father had his limits: One Sunday morning there were two guys hanging around the boat with my dad. They were minister's sons and kind of sneaking away from church. So my dad gave them a cold pop to drink and they were sitting there in the sun feeling alright. But then my dad got some water from the coal bin in a bucket and snuck around and doused them with it. He said to them, "Go home and explain how you got that on your white Sunday shirts."

Once in a while, my dad would take me on the big boat and bring me to meet Captain Bob-lo. He would give me one of those huge all-day suckers. A couple of times his wife was with him. She was a little person too. She would wear a dress with flowers on it, and they would go walking hand in hand onto the island.

My father would do odd jobs at Troy Browning's house in Amherstburg. He sent him to Toronto to get his wheelsman's license. One thing Bob-lo didn't have for their employees was a pension plan. If you didn't save on your own, you were out of luck. My father would have to apply for his job every year. There were other people who wanted his job but never were able to take it from him.

I worked in the cafeteria in 1963. When I was younger, it was off limits to blacks and my dad just told me that was someplace I shouldn't go. I got married in 1964 then came back in 1965 to work in *the souvenir shop with Mrs. Browning and worked until 1973 in various concession jobs. During that time they brought Motown performers over to the dance hall. Marvin Gaye, Stevie Wonder, the Spinners, and the Four Tops all performed. The crowds weren't much, and I didn't realize I was watching history at the time.*

When I left Bob-lo, I left Bob-lo. It was enough for me. I made a lot of nice friends and still see them over the years. A couple of years ago I went to a school reunion there with some friends. But we were restricted to the dance hall and couldn't look around the island.[11]

Cliff Thompson (left) and deckhand on the Maudie. *Photograph courtesy Gerald Pattenden.*

In September 1956 *Billboard Magazine* noted another longstanding tradition, as "the final return trip from Bob-lo of the *Columbia* on Labor Day, the traditional last day of the season, is greeted by illuminated spray salutes, flashing lights and sirens from the Amherstburg fire trucks parked along the river front." On those rare nights, the Joe Vitale Quartet perched on the top deck behind the pilot house and played "Auld Lang Syne" as the *Columbia* slowly proceeded close to the Canadian shore, its whistle growing hoarse blowing an endless salute—three long and two short—to what seemed like the entire population of the city of Amherstburg gathered along the waterfront. It was a bittersweet farewell of lovers looking forward to warm days in the future when they would be reunited.

(Opposite page, top)
The Maudie at the island work dock. Courtesy Elizabeth Thompson in honor of Clifford Thompson.

(Opposite page, bottom)
The Amherstburg ferry C. E. Park *was named after the celebrated Bob-lo employee. Photograph courtesy Dossin Great Lakes Museum, Detroit, Michigan.*

The island ca. 1956.
In author's collection.

On May 28, 1957, the U.S. Army Corps of Engineers began its project to deepen the Amherstburg Channel to St. Lawrence Seaway standards, opening the Great Lakes to the world. For the entire season, boat passengers were treated to the sight of the barges and booms employed by the Corps as they dynamited and then dredged the channel out to the Detroit River Light. The river bottom they dredged was dumped on an area starting at the southern end of Bob-lo and extending over a mile into the lake. A vein of sand running across the mouth of the river was dredged and dumped on the spit and created the area known today as White Sands. Dredging material was also used to expand the small islet off the northern end that became known as the Horseshoe anchorage.[12]

That summer Bob-lo took a great leap forward in the Detroit amusement world with the addition of three new rides: the Wild Mouse, the Satellite Jets, and the Scrambler. These rides represented a significant shift from the quiet, passive recreation park to a twentieth-century amusement park. The Wild Mouse alone was a major attraction, and suddenly Jefferson Beach, Walled Lake, and Edgewater began to appear dated to the new generation of thrill-seeking baby boomers.

Yet it was a blend of the old with the new that helped Bob-lo post a net increase for the 1957 season in spite of several weeks of cold, rainy weather that resulted in a decline in attendance. The key to this gain was more per capita spending, and what better place to spend some

The dredge Hornet *and barge as seen from the* Columbia. *Photograph courtesy Art Herrala Collection, Macomb Township, Michigan.*

money than the venerable roller rink? Opened in 1940 in the stone building that originally housed the carousel, the rink had increased its business by 5 percent for the year. The gain was credited to a personalized management system that paid careful attention to operating policies. Also, the rink was sheltered, and skating was a great way to keep warm on an otherwise miserable day. An ample spectator balcony that provided both shelter and promotion to potential skaters drew hundreds more to the building. One *Billboard* article told of several girls arriving after the rink had closed for the day. Park superintendent Harold Gorry took them to the dance hall, where he provided them a place to skate and free music on the jukebox. The rink staff was composed of ten people—a manager, a cashier, two skate room boys, two floor men, and four skate boys. The article closed with a glowing account of the personalized attention that was devoted to every phase of the operation, citing Superintendent Gorry's willingness to fill in wherever help was needed.[13]

By the end of the 1957 season, the park boasted eighteen adult rides and eight kiddie rides plus the ponies. Bob-lo also hosted the St. Andrews festival for the fiftieth time. Although Walter Campbell had been gone for over thirty years, this event was still the only one to be granted a liquor license on the island, and that just for the day. In homage to the spirit of Campbell, who invested heavily in island beautification, the park also employed six full-time gardeners.

The newly created White Sands area on the island's south end became an overnight headache to the Brownings, who witnessed increased incursions and vandalism to the island as a result of pleasure boaters flocking to the new recreation site. There were repeated break-ins to the old lighthouse, which had already lost its lamproom to a fire set by vandals in 1954.[14]

In the following decade, the Brownings bought up ninety acres of land along the river in Amherstburg and began mining that same vein of sand for sale to the glass industry. However, when the sand was found to contain traces of iron, the venture was abandoned, and the land became the site for a new Amherstburg dock and parking lot, built in the late 1960s.[15]

Bob-lo Profiles: Under the Influence of Bob-lo

Another sign of changing times occurred early in the season, when a committee of Detroit Eastern High School students, including Art Carter, planned their 1958 senior class trip:

> *These days, a lot of high school groups plan for Florida, the Caribbean, or Mexico for their senior trips. Back then, it was an adventure for us to go somewhere like Bob-lo. I was social chairman of our class, and we decided that's where we would go. It sounds quaint today, but for us it was a far off place. Although many of my classmates had been there and I had been on the boat, I had never been to Bob-lo Island before. That was the first time I had a chance to really spend time on the water.*

I clearly remember the trip sailing down the river, and once we got there we had a real adventure going around the island to the rides. Although some of us had heard about the park's history of excluding blacks to certain days, we really didn't think about it back then. We were more concerned with having fun on that one day. For me and my friends, it was a chance to get away from the everyday life of academics and to fantasize about taking a cruise to some exotic place around the world. That exotic place ended up being Bob-lo Island in 1958.

One of my friends and I would design boats for a fantasy trip around the world, and the Bob-lo trip became one of our experiments toward that end. That particular trip to Bob-lo encouraged my lifelong fascination with boating and water and eventually inspired me to want to create some type of educational experience for kids around the water and boating. Several years later I purchased the Renaissance Queen *and ran tours along the Detroit River. In the 1990s I became director of the Sankore Maritime Academy in Detroit.*[16]

In May of 1958 the management announced additions to the park, including a two-and-a-half-mile railway that would go around the island. They also brought in a two-hundred-year-old band organ imported from Germany to be operated as free entertainment for park visitors. It was confirmed that the independently owned excursion vessel *Canadiana* would make runs to the park from Toledo. The cruise took two and a half hours aboard the twenty-five-hundred-passenger vessel, significantly increasing the park's potential capacity. The round trip fare was set at $2.50.

The park also planned to unveil a new fun-in-the-dark ride and to relocate the Kiddieland to a more shaded area near the merry-go-round. The addition of the new rides meant a need for increased power. In June of 1958 it was announced that all power to the island was now being provided by Ontario Hydro through a submarine cable. After half a century of service, the island powerhouse was shut down. Twenty-five years after the Ferry Company first proposed the idea, the park was for the first time running on alternating current.[17]

On July 1 the company had every sailing stop in Windsor to help boost attendance on the Dominion Day holiday. Under this arrangement, boats loaded passengers first in Detroit and then headed across the river, where those passengers went through Canadian customs before the boat loaded the Windsor passengers for the trip to Bob-lo. Immigration officials were amused to discover that, when they asked the routine question "Where were you born?" many Detroiters automatically answered, "Bob-lo."[18]

Later that month, park revenue was up by 10 percent. This was in spite of flat attendance, indicating that per capita spending was up, an unexpected outcome in a period of unemployment and recession. Gorry attributed the upsurge to the new train ride and to an intensive promotional campaign to market the park to groups for picnics. The anticipated spike in attendance brought by the *Canadiana* had been offset by the fact that the ship was only able to stay at the park a few hours before boarding passengers for the return to Toledo. Yet another special was unveiled when a trainload of passengers from Shiawassee and Clinton counties arrived at the Bob-lo docks as part of a pay-one-price train and boat promotion.[19]

On July 30, returning to Toledo in the Maumee River, the *Canadiana* hit a drawbridge. Although there were no serious injuries among the nine hundred passengers, the superstructure of the ship was badly damaged and the ship was forced to withdraw from the Bob-lo service for the year. Although an effort was made to revive the service the next year, a tarnished reputation and rainy weekends made the *Canadiana* an unprofitable venture. The once proud Crystal Beach steamer be-

The Canadiana *at island dock. Photograph courtesy Dossin Great Lakes Museum, Detroit, Michigan.*

came an itinerant of Lake Erie ports from that time on, never returning to the excursion trade that she had engaged in for almost half a
century.[20]

Bob-lo Profiles: Bob-lo's Most Wanted

Leroy's Back in Jail Again

Amherstburg resident Denise Bondy recalls a day on Bob-lo unlike most
others:

> In 1959, there was a robbery attempted on the island. Someone tipped
> the police beforehand, so my father was over there. The island was
> policed by Ontario Provincial Police (OPP) because it was part of
> Malden Township, not the city of Amherstburg. If anything serious
> happened, the local police would have to go because the OPP only
> had one person for the district and that person was stationed outside
> of town.
>
> A local group of people from Amherstburg planned it. They in-
> cluded Leroy Morency, who was a local kid who came from a dysfunc-
> tional family and [was] always in trouble. He was a daredevil who
> would swim out to the Bob-lo boat with some of the others as it was
> coming past and hang onto the under railstrakes and ride the boat
> into the island. The captain would be blowing the whistle to get those
> kids away, but it wouldn't stop them. As Leroy got older, he got in
> bigger trouble and became pretty notorious in these parts. The singer
> from Windsor Jack Scott recorded a song called "Leroy's Back in Jail
> Again" after one of his escapades made the papers.
>
> The gang on the island actually had guns at a time when no one
> used guns around here. The police staked out the Women's Cottage
> on the island. The cottage was used as a place for the park managers
> to keep money at night when they couldn't make a bank deposit. The
> gang knew this, as did the informer who tipped the police to the plan.
>
> It was night. The police staked out the cottage; the robbery took
> place; shots were fired; and my father ended up with a bullet hole in
> his hat. There was a chase, and Leroy disappeared into the woods,
> jumped into the water, and swam to Grosse Ile. The police, worried
> that he was still in the woods, threatened to close the island until he
> was found. After a few days he came back to Amherstburg and sur-
> rendered. He had enough against him that he was sent to prison—
> this time in Kingston.

He came back in 1968 and showed up to visit my father, who was in retirement by then. Leroy apologized and said he was going to go straight and didn't want to return to prison. My father was skeptical because he knew Leroy from when he was a kid. But he'd have Leroy come and cut firewood for him and do other things my dad could no longer do.

Leroy made good on his commitment and eventually got married. He was able to find work and make a living. One of the things he liked to do was dive, and he often helped the authorities in recovering cars that ended up in the river. One day a car went in off the foot of Murray Street with a young girl driving. The police divers weren't successful in their attempts to get to the car, so Leroy went down there. But his equipment got tangled up somehow, and he died.[21]

The Browning brothers worked hard to cultivate the goodwill of the communities that they served. Bill Browning had at least one thing in common with Walter Campbell—they both believed that Bob-lo should be for families. Browning extended this philosophy to treat his staff as family so that they would, in turn, treat their guests the same way. One major difference between Campbell and Browning was in their relationship to political figures in Windsor and Detroit. While Campbell was notorious for his tactics of bluffs, threats, and feuding with mayors and councilmen, Browning's strategy was to become closely involved with civic affairs to aid his business relationships. Browning was named by Mayor Louis Miriani to co-chair the first Freedom Festival in Detroit. He got to know the mayor of Windsor and worked with leaders in Amherstburg to address issues related to employment of blacks on the island.

The Brownings also worked hard to keep the crew of their ships and office staff happy. They maintained good working relationships with the unions, including the Musicians, Seafarers International Union (SIU), and Masters Mates and Pilots Union. In their thirty-one years of ownership, they had to shut the business early only one year, when crew members walked off in sympathy to the firing of a second mate. There were times when actions went beyond just sympathy. Bill Browning recalled a meeting with a crewman and the agent for the SIU. The crewman said something that the agent took exception to, and "[the agent] came across the room and belted the man right off his chair."[22]

The cramped living conditions aboard both the *Columbia* and *Ste. Claire* were a constant source of concern to crew members who were required to be aboard to maintain a full safety contingent during all cruises per Coast Guard regulations. While the newer *Ste. Claire* had a bit more space thanks to captain and mate quarters located adjacent the pilot house, many of the *Columbia*'s crew were cramped below decks in scenes that would be familiar to those who immigrated to the United States in steerage class in the early 1900s. The Brownings gave crews from both ships permission to sleep at home if they chose to, although they were not allowed to leave until the ships had finished their cruises for the day. With the popularity of the moonlight trade expanding, this often meant that a ship was not back in her berth until after midnight. The good news was that they only had to put up with these accommodations for the ninety-day season from Memorial Day to Labor Day. To further compensate, the Brownings went out of

Photograph courtesy Dossin Great Lakes Museum, Detroit, Michigan.

their way to ensure that the galleys aboard the two ships acquired the reputation among sailors as the finest on the Great Lakes—a perk that helped ensure a committed, professional crew.

Another example of the Brownings' commitment to family business was found in their policy that promised safe delivery of children. One time a group of kids from Saginaw could not get on the boat coming

back from the island because of overcrowding of the four o'clock boat. Bill Browning recalls, "That happened a lot—there were days when more people wanted to go back on the four o'clock than we could get on the boat. We'd load the ship to capacity and then close the gates. Whoever was left on the dock would have to wait for the next boat to arrive at 5:30. So this group of kids, by the time they got back to the Detroit dock, had missed their ride home. So, when I heard about it, I put them in a cab all the way to Saginaw."[23]

The company's community outreach efforts were highlighted when the park opened with a private preview for crippled children on May 29 under the sponsorship of the Rotary Club. The event was the result of a collaboration between the Brownings and bandleader Joe Vitale and hosted eight hundred children.[24]

Bob-lo Profiles: The Bandleader

Joe Vitale was born in 1920 and trained as a show drummer. He worked on the road in Ohio and New York until 1950, when he hired on with Bob-lo to manage the bands on the Columbia *and* Ste. Claire. *Besides managing the ship orchestras and drumming on the* Columbia, *he worked all the big theaters downtown over the rest of the year as well as the Shrine Circus. He met his wife, a chorus dancer, while doing a show at the Latin Quarter. His gregarious, outgoing personality made him friends everywhere he went, and he was happy to be able to stay in the Detroit area to make his living.*

During the 1960s, he played on recording sessions for Stevie Wonder, the Supremes, and the Temptations.

As the boat departed the Detroit dock, Joe's tradition was to haul his show drum up to the third deck and accompany his men playing "Sailing Sailing" and "Anchors Aweigh" while Captain Bob-lo would dance on the dock below. On day cruises coming back from the island, the daily favorites were "The Mexican Hat Dance" and "The Hokey Pokey." On moonlight cruises, Joe's signature last song was "Goodnight Ladies."

One of Joe's children was born with a handicap and was a resident at the St. Louis Center in Chelsea. Joe, who served on the center's board, arranged with Bill Browning to have an opening day preview on Bob-lo for the residents and thus established a long-standing tradition.

One evening in the late fifties, Joe went to help someone who jumped over the side of the Columbia. He climbed down the side and threw a life ring to the person in the water. He hurt his back in the process and had back pain the rest of his life from that incident.

On one Sunday during the July 1967 riots, Joe helped to calm the passengers returning from Bob-lo while buses were rounded up at the dock to safely transport them out of the city.

Bill Browning remembers,

Joe was very important to the operation. He was the most friendly, outgoing company guy. He'd help out any way he could. He even served as a bartender on the boat when we got crowded. He helped to resolve union issues with band members. He was a very significant part of the operation. On the last trip of every season from the island, he had his band up on the top deck playing to the crowds bidding farewell from Amherstburg. Of course, he was also trying to keep an eye on the Amherstburg kids riding the big boat back to the city. They could get rambunctious on that trip.

And Ralph Browning recalls, "He was personable and professional and put in incredible hours. Sometimes he was there finishing a moonlight at 1 AM and back on that same morning for a Canadian Day at 7 AM. He was like one of the family."

Joe reserved the top deck of the Columbia for VIPs and friends on the night of the Freedom Festival fireworks. He carried his public persona below decks, where he was a regular in the crew's poker game. He also invested in a few of the island rides.

In the mid 1970s, Joe convinced the Brownings to offer big bands on the moonlights, offering to personally guarantee their success. That helped revitalize the moonlights. He worked the boats for thirty-three years, until the

bands were replaced by other forms of entertainment. Joe continued to promote the big band sound that was his passion first at Metro Beach and then
at other venues in the area. He always brought a big band back to the boats
for a moonlight, sometimes several times a season. Joe played the homecom-
ing at the Detroit Athletic Club in 1999 and died a month later.[25]

*Joe Vitale (playing drums) and his band
on the third deck. Photograph courtesy
Walter P. Reuther Library, Wayne State
University, Detroit, Michigan.*

The white Bob-Lo vessels form the largest fleet of International Excursion boats in America. Each is designed to give you the fullest measure of fun and enjoyment. Aboard you'll find refreshment counters, clean rest rooms, deck chairs and dancing every trip to the music of the ships orchestra, along with many other accommodations for your comfort and relaxation.

SMALL GROUP . . . OR LARGE!
Daytime . . . or Starlight!

BOB-LO
brings you the perfect answer for your
GROUP OUTINGS

Printed in U.S.A.

BOB-LO
STARLIGHT CRUISE

**BOB-LO STARLIGHT CRUISE DEPARTS
FROM FOOT OF WOODWARD AVE. EVERY NIGHT
(EXCEPT MONDAYS) AT 9:00 P.M.**

(SATURDAY NIGHTS AT 9:00 P.M. AND 10:00 P.M.)
Friday and Saturday Nights a Ninety Minute Stop
at Bob-Lo Island Park.
FARE $1.75 PER PERSON

★ TWILIGHT CRUISE ★

DEPARTS DETROIT	AT	6:00 P.M.
BACK IN DETROIT	AT	10:30 P.M.

Adults.......$1.50 Roundtrip – Child...... .75 Roundtrip
NO 6:00 P.M. SAILINGS ON FRIDAYS

GREATEST FUN VALUE IN AMERICA
It's Cool – Comfortable – Exciting
Go in the Daylight————————Return in the Starlight
And romance on the starlit river aboard the luxurious
BOB-LO STEAMER
Free Dancing on Shipboard – Dinner at the Island
*Wonderful Food – Graciously Served in Cool, Inviting
Surroundings – at Popular Prices*
GET UP A PARTY – GO WITH A FRIEND – GO ALONE –
Nowhere can you have as much fun, for such a small cost.

THIS IS BOB-LO
THE INTERNATIONAL PLAYGROUND

And this is your personal invitation to
COME TO BOB-LO - - -

SEE DETROIT AND WINDSOR
SKYLINE ★ ★ ★ ★ from comfortable deck
chairs on wide breeze-swept decks ★ ★ ★ from
spotless, oil-fueled ships.

★ ★ ★

40 MILE BOAT RIDE ON THE
WORLD'S BUSIEST WATERWAY . . .

★ ★ ★

240 ACRES OF WOODED

PLAYLAND IS YOUR
DESTINATION

SEASON MEMORIAL DAY THRU LABOR DAY

BOB-LO

DOCK & TICKET OFFICE
FOOT OF WOODWARD AVE.
PHONE WO 2-9622
DETROIT — MICH.

One of the spotless white Bob-Lo boats returning to Detroit.

The fabulous new Satellite Jet – only one of the importations from Germany for Bob-Lo and you.

Bob-Lo scenic Railroad takes you to the far end of the Island, past the modern Amusement Zone, historic Block House, Light House, and Sailors Memorial.

The fun begins when you arrive at the dock and Captain Bob-Lo takes over.

BOB-LO
THE INTERNATIONAL PLAYGROUND

★ One of the thrilling experiences every visitor to Detroit looks forward to is the Bob-Lo excursion — the exciting 18-mile ride to Detroit's famous island playground. Every year visitors from all over the world join the tens of thousands of Detroiters in this gala excursion. Last year over a half million people enjoyed this unforgettable day cruising on the river. You see ships of all types plowing along the busiest river in the world. You see Detroit as it can be seen at its best — from the river — the skyscrapers standing tall against the sky, the immense spread of Detroit's fabulous industries, mile after mile along the river bank. And on the other side you see Canada, the cities and farms of a friendly neighbor nation.

★ What's more, it is all so very gay. The band plays. The voyageurs dance or relax in the deck chairs. They wave at the passing ships. They point out the unusual landmarks. And then you are at famous, breezy Bob-Lo, Detroit's summer playground.

★ This beautiful island — all 240 acres — is rich in recreational facilities. Playgrounds, a spacious dining room, 5,000 picnic tables and benches, the latest in amusement rides, everything you would desire for a glorious holiday. Many loiter until dusk on this pleasant island so they can come home at night with the river bank ablaze with lights and the leaping flames from huge industries creating an unforgettable picture. This river holiday is one of the highlights of any visit to Detroit.

An International Tribute to the Sailors of the Great Lakes.

You dance on the breeze-swept dance floor to the music of a popular orchestra.

Nowhere, except from the deck of a Bob-Lo steamer, can you get a close-up view of the giant lake freighters on the Detroit River.

WHY NOT LET A BOB-LO REPRESENTATIVE HELP YOU PLAN YOUR NEXT OUTING !

In 1960 Ken Capstick replaced Harold Gorry as park superinten-dent. He took over as the island park entered a new era of amusement rides and began to attract a steady and growing clientele. The attrac-tion of the rides, led by the Wild Mouse and Satellite Jets, eclipsed the roller rink and silent, cavernous dance hall. In 1961 the old island dock was replaced with a unique new dock comprised of the sunken hull of a freighter formerly known as the *Queenston*.

In 1962 it looked like Bill Browning's political work would pay off when the Detroit Common Council approved construction of a new dock at the foot of Woodward and a ten-year lease with a promise for public parking as well. But then new council member Anthony Wi-erzbicki, upset at what he perceived as a sweetheart deal, countered with a proposal to remove the entire Bob-lo facility from the city, effec-tively killing the proposal. The island itself provided some good news, however, as it recorded its best attendance since 1955, with 580,000 customers.[26]

In 1963, the Rolly Hoop and Flight to Mars were added to the park's growing stable of rides. Fred Smitka became the new rides supervisor on the island. Smitka first hired on with the Brownings in 1949 to work on the steamers and rose to the role of fleet superintendent. He stayed on at the park until the Brownings divested their freighter op-erations in 1965 and then became a marine consultant involved in in-spections of the ferry fleets under new owners until the island closed in 1993.[27]

During the following season, the Port-O-Call Marina was opened on the west side of the island to the world of private boating so abun-dant in the region. The Brownings also made news with a proposal for an auto race course for the north end of the island that was never realized. Radio station CKLW placed a small trailer on the island for live mobile broadcasts.

(Opposite page)
Courtesy Dossin Great Lakes Museum, Detroit, Michigan.

Bob-lo Profiles: The Big Eight

Dave Shafer Show on CKLW
Live From Bob-lo Island
August 1964—A Saturday

Jingle: CKLW Million Dollar Music
Intro Song

Dave Shafer: Hi. Good Afternoon, everybody. This is Dave Shafer coming to you from beautiful Bob-lo Island. It's a gorgeous day out here. Got music for you until 5:45. So let's get under way and do some swinging through the afternoon at CKLW, home of the Happy Fellas.

Out Intro

Song: "Pretty Woman"

DS: That's Roy Orbison. "Pretty Woman." Starting the day off for you on the Dave Shafer show. It's a gorgeous day out here. Seventy-two degrees.

Ad: Michigan State Fair promo.

Ad: CKLW record hops for Lakeshore Park, Kingsville (Dave Shafer), Allie's Resort at Wamplers Lake (Joe Van) and K of C Hall in Mt. Clemens.

Ad: Stagecoach West starting this fall on TV 9.

Jingle: CKLW Swings

DS: Here comes Roger Miller now entertaining on the Dave Shafer show with "Chug a Lug." Whoop whoop whoop . . .

Song: "Chug-a-lug"

DS: That's Roger Miller with a good sound here on CK.

Ad: Food Fair [DS] "Have you tried Food Fair Meats . . ."

Jingle: Radio Eight Oh CKLW

Ad: A Hard Day's Night film promo [DS] "Now showing at these theaters . . ."

Jingle: Everyone's listening to CKLW

DS: Something new from the Kingsmen. "Death of an Angel."

Song: "Death of an Angel"

DS: That's something new from the Kingsmen called "Death of an Angel," and its something new on this week's CK survey. . . . Baby please come home . . .

Ad: Silver Cup [DS] "Not one, not two, but three great shapes . . .

Jingle: CKLW

DS: Weatherman says partly cloudy today, high of 78. Low 60. Warmer tomorrow with a high in the low 80s. Pollen count is only 55 today. That's low compared to the past few days. Water temps: Lake St. Clair 66, Lake Erie is 69 degrees. It's seventeen after two, and we bring you the sound of Mr. Gene Pitney. "It Hurts to Be in Love." Gene . . .

Song: "It Hurts to Be in Love"

DS: That's Gene Pitney. Down to number 7 this week on the CK survey with "It Hurts to Be in Love," and it's a gorgeous day out there. Seventy-two degrees, and I feel like jumping in the river off the pier here at Bob-lo Island. It's nineteen and a half after two, and I'll have no cheering back at the studio for that. . . . As I mentioned, nineteen and a half after two o'clock, and I'm here on Bob-lo all day for you![28]

In 1964 the *Detroit Free Press* compared the 1949 season—the Brownings' first—to the upcoming one. In 1949 there were only three hundred group picnics booked compared to more than one thousand already booked for 1964. Similarly, the 1964 season again projected more than 600,000 visitors, double that from fifteen years previous. Overall revenue nearly doubled over that period, with rides now accounting for 70 percent of the volume and food and miscellaneous activities earning the remaining 30 percent—a significant change from the late 1920s. The Detroit steamers also ferried another sixty thousand passengers a year on charter and Saturday moonlight cruises that did not go to the island. Again sounding much like Walter Campbell, Bill Browning was quoted as saying, "We consider this primarily a family and picnic park. We have nothing that will not pass the test of good taste with family or church groups."[29] Rates for school groups were promoted at one dollar per student, with free transportation and lunch thrown in for teachers.[30] Of course, besides paying the ten-cent admission fee to the island, visitors would be charged an additional amount for each of the rides. Aided by twenty-seven days hotter than ninety degrees, Bob-lo finished the 1964 season 20 percent ahead of the previous year.[31]

The 1965 season initiated Teen Fair Days, which featured Detroit rock and soul groups on the boats and in the dance hall. Radio and television personality Robin Seymour conducted live remote broadcasts from the dance hall on the island that included the Rationals, Barbara Lewis, and Martha and the Vandellas.[32]

However, that summer season was marred by two incidents. On the first Canadian Day, a fight erupted in the dance hall between twenty white Canadian auto workers and a group of blacks from the United States. In response, the Ontario Human Rights Commission investigating charges of discrimination in hiring practices of several Amherstburg businesses included Bob-lo in their hearings. Their findings called for a change in hiring policy to employ more blacks at the island.[33]

Then, in late August, the Bug ran off its rail, killing one rider and injuring eight others, three critically. The accident made headlines in Detroit and Windsor, and an investigation revealed that there were no municipal or provincial laws regulating amusement ride safety in Ontario. The ride operator at the time of the accident was a sixteen-year-old boy from Amherstburg. A subsequent probe cited metal fatigue as the cause.[34] In spite of the dramatic headlines and graphic pictures in the papers, there was no indication that island business slackened as a result. The island and boats continued to prosper in the 1960s.

Along with the rest of the city, the company experienced a setback when, in 1967, the operation was shut down for a week during the Detroit riots. The riots, precipitated by a predawn police raid on an illegal black drinking establishment, provoked several days of mayhem that engulfed entire neighborhoods on both the east and west sides of the city and left over forty dead. The ships were ordered away from the docks by the fire commissioner on the first night—a Sunday—when rumors began circulating about mobs coming downtown to burn them. The *Columbia* and *Ste. Claire* went to the Ojibway anchorage downriver for several nights and returned to the docks every morning only to pick up provisions and head back to the anchorage.

Aside from the lost week at anchor, the aftermath of the riots did not have a serious effect on the operation, as thousands of shocked Detroiters tried to return to normalcy as quickly as possible. Since Bob-lo was already well established as a summertime getaway from the worries of city life, it was natural for people to close their eyes to the burned out buildings along Gratiot and Grand River and go to the dock that would take them away from the city, at least for a day. The island continued to attract steady, if not overflowing, numbers of Detroiters for the duration of the season. At least one of the ships was booked as a charter every night by groups of churches, clubs, and businesses, including Motown Records.[35]

In 1968 the outstate train/boat trip was successfully revived, and the Skydiver and Swiss Bob rides were installed. With attendance for 1968 just shy of seven hundred thousand, Bill and Red Browning looked to Amherstburg to expand the Bob-lo operation.[36] They oversaw construction of a new dock and parking for eight hundred cars on their Amherstburg property, in part to continue diversifying transportation to the island and also in anticipation of extending operating dates into September. The newly built *Windmill Point* ferry with a capacity of 118 passengers was put into service from that site, replacing the tiny *C. E. Park*. Although Jefferson Beach had been closed for several years, the Brownings' operation was still competing locally with Edgewater Park and Walled Lake. Cedar Point on Lake Erie in nearby Ohio had been in a long-term rebuilding phase since 1959 and was successfully attracting thousands of southeast Michigan residents. Faced with the prospect of being turned into a residential resort community, Cedar Point owners elected to build a causeway that directly linked the park to nearby Sandusky, thereby eliminating the problems associated with travel by ship and significantly expanding its market. As a result, attendance at that park had spiked to 2.5 million by 1969.[37] It had been several years since Cedar Point unveiled its Blue Streak coaster, and the Brownings were acutely aware of the need to build a marquee coaster for Bob-lo. Unfortunately, the premier coaster builder, the Philadelphia Toboggan Company, citing the skyrocketing cost of treated southern pine for a wooden coaster, strongly advised against such an investment on Bob-lo.[38]

The 1969 season zoomed into view, and, instead of a new coaster, the company announced construction of a new Adventure Land Zoo. The $400,000 zoo occupied the site south of the dock just above where the original cafeteria hung over the banks of the river. The zoo was designed to allow the miniature train to pass through it. A brochure for the zoo proclaimed, "Nothing's created so much excitement since the Indians held forth at Bob-lo." The five new rides announced for the year—the most ever introduced in one season—included the Sky Hi Slide, the Monster, sports cars, Alpine Ski Lift, and Sky Diver. Kiddieland got a new junior coaster and two umbrella rides. Bill Browning reported that bookings for picnics and charters were again up. As

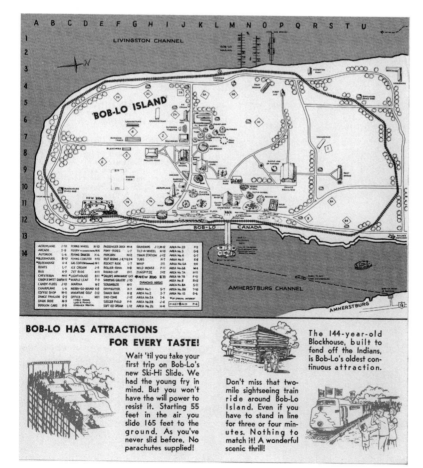

BOB-LO HAS ATTRACTIONS FOR EVERY TASTE!

Wait 'til you take your first trip on Bob-lo's new Ski-Hi Slide. We had the young fry in mind. But you won't have the will power to resist it. Starting 55 feet in the air you slide 165 feet to the ground. As you've never slid before. No parachutes supplied!

Don't miss that two-mile sightseeing train ride around Bob-Lo Island. Even if you have to stand in line for three or four minutes. Nothing to match it! A wonderful scenic thrill!

The 144-year-old Blockhouse, built to fend off the Indians, is Bob-lo's oldest continuous attraction.

A map of Bob-lo in the late 1960s featuring the new zoo. Courtesy Dossin Great Lakes Museum, Detroit, Michigan.

the Bob-lo makeover continued, the old Moon Rocket and Caterpillar were listed for sale at bargain basement prices of $3,500 each.[39]

In early May 1970 an announcement was made that the company had settled with the family of Laurence Baudin, eighteen, who was injured in the Bug derailment in 1965 and died after three years of being unconscious. The $1 million suit was settled for $200,000, although the park did not concede negligence.

The island increased its ride lineup to thirty-six with the addition of a new Caterpillar, Meteor, and Swiss Toboggan ride, the latter two owned and operated by W. G. Wade Shows. Ten thousand dollars was reinvested in the island's first ride, the vintage carousel. Ten-cent tickets were now in regular use for all rides, and hopes for a million visitor year were floated by management.[40] Responding to rumors that the island would change its hiring policy and only employ college students, Superintendent Capstick said that there would be no change and that Amherstburg youth would still be favored for employment on the island. To keep his options open, he also expressed the need for safety—especially in ride operation—and noted that most high schoolers were not available for work until the second or third week of June. For 1971 the boat ride from Detroit to Bob-lo cost $2.50. The company introduced an all-day ride ticket for an additional $4.00, although individual ride tickets were still widely in use. For Labor Day, the Bob-lo Line partnered with the Michigan Railroad Club to offer a Blue Water Boat Train cruise to Port Huron.[41]

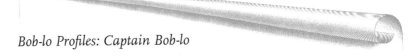

Bob-lo Profiles: Captain Bob-lo

Joe Short was the company mascot, the midget known as Captain Bob-lo. He started in show business at the age of fourteen, long before he came to work for the Brownings in 1955. Before coming to Bob-lo, he worked his way up to a clown position with Ringling Brothers Circus. Princess Louise, another performer of the stage, became his wife and would sometimes accompany him to Bob-lo.

Ralph Browning remembers, "The kids loved the way he would prance on the dock while Joe Vitale and the band played 'Anchors Away' as the Columbia *got under way for Bob-lo. He was a constant reminder that this was an amusement business and that everyone—workers and customers alike—should be enjoying themselves."*

Joe once said of himself, "I suppose I'm the richest man in the world. Not in money, but inside when I hear laughter from kids. That's great for my morale and I feel rich."

After the Bob-lo season ended, Joe would work as a Santa's helper or elf at Kern's or Hudson's. He was also a regular with the Shrine Circus when it came to town.

The owner of Jumbo's Bar on Selden and Third gave them an apartment in a house next door to the bar. It was fitted out with miniature furniture, with a couch three and a half feet long and a tiny matching rocker nearby.

Off the boats, Joe liked to relax like every working man. According to Browning, "His wife, Princess Louise, knew he liked to drink his martinis. So she'd show up down at the docks on payday and take his check before he could cash it. He didn't like it."

"When Joe got up in years, we let him set his own schedule for the Bob-lo boats," says Bill Browning. "He would usually be there, but it was up to him how long he would stay or whether he would take the boat to the island, which he sometimes did."

After Princess Louise died in 1968, Joe became distraught, and the evidence of old age began to creep up on him. He died before Christmas 1974, a year after he stopped working for Bob-lo. He was ninety-one.[42]

Captain Bob-lo, Joe Short, and his wife, Princess Louise, May 1966. Photograph courtesy Art Herrala Collection.

In 1972 Bob-lo benefited from the demise of a Canadian entrepreneur's short-lived Peche Island park venture by acquiring three boats and renaming them the *Papoose III, Papoose IV,* and *Papoose V.* The boats became the nucleus of the Amherstburg ferry fleet, joining the *Windmill Pointe.* The new vessels each had a capacity of 275 passengers. The Amherstburg docks had finally acquired the capacity to transport up to 10,000 people per day.[43]

Behind the scenes, the island acceded to the request of the Ontario Water Resources Commission and added an oxidation system to the wastewater lagoon in place since 1915. The lagoon was located close to the north end of the island, well away from the amusement area.[44]

The amusement wars continued on as the company invested two million dollars and rolled out a brand new Sansui steel roller coaster and a log flume. Although the coaster did not rival the new wooden Gemini unveiled earlier at Cedar Point, it helped maintain island attendance. The antique cars and swan boats also made their debut that year, when organized groups again accounted for 60 percent of the park's visitors.[45]

With a one-price system that included the ferry, admission to the park, and ride tickets now firmly in place, 1974 was heralded as a banner year for the park with attendance approaching the 750,000 mark. The new Hofbrau restaurant became the first establishment licensed to serve alcohol in the history of Bob-lo. A renovated East Coast ship, renamed the *City of Wyandotte,* with a capacity of thirteen hundred passengers, was added to the fleet exclusively to ferry passengers from Wyandotte every day. Previously, the *Columbia* or *Ste. Claire* would stop in Wyandotte en route to Bob-lo on their morning runs on selected days and drop passengers there in the evening. On busy days, this meant that the boat from Detroit could not load to full capacity, sometimes leaving frustrated passengers on the dock. The island attracted over 700,000 visitors the previous year with 200,000 coming directly through Amherstburg and the remainder aboard the *Columbia* and *Ste. Claire* in Detroit and Wyandotte. "We couldn't carry everyone who wanted to go out of Detroit last year," said Bill Browning explaining the new ship purchase to a reporter. "We're expecting 125,000 persons to use our Wyandotte site the first year."[46]

The Browning management team was confronting a problem that had confounded their predecessors. Since the construction of the Ambassador Bridge and Windsor Tunnel, there were viable, less expensive alternatives than to get to Bob-lo by boat from Detroit. The cost of maintaining the large steamers ate up a sizeable chunk of the Bob-lo operating budget. The wages for the crews and musicians and the insurance for the boats made it difficult to turn a profit year in and year out. The Brownings felt that they could realize a better net profit by operating smaller ferries exclusively out of Wyandotte and Amherstburg but feared that doing away with the big boats and Detroit docks would diminish the visibility and attractiveness of Bob-lo for the Detroit market. Bill Browning explained, "We couldn't stand still. Bob-lo used to be known primarily for the boat ride. Now we want to be known as an amusement center. We've still got a lot of room for expansion. Bob-lo's a two-hundred-acre island, and we're only using fifty acres now. We've got a lot more land than any park I know of."[47]

The *City of Wyandotte* proved a difficult boat. Unmanageable in the wind, she had all sorts of problems, including smoke emissions and steerage. One afternoon the steering gear broke near the Bob-lo Island dock, and the ship drifted across the river and hit an old ship's pilot house sitting on the lawn of a house in Amherstburg. The ship became known as the "CoW" among her crew and lasted only two seasons.[48]

On the island, plans for expanding the amusement sector faced additional challenges. The *Windsor Star* and other papers pointed to an accident on the Scrambler in which a mother and daughter were injured and used it to highlight the fact that, over the past ten years, fifteen people had been injured in accidents on the carousel, Bug, and Wild Mouse.[49]

The following winter, the city of Detroit announced plans to build the new Hart Plaza on the riverfront. The Bob-lo building was demolished, and the docks at the foot of Woodward were relocated to the foot of Third Street behind Cobo Hall. While the city paid the Brownings $500,000 for the property and accommodated the company by creating a parking turnaround and signage to direct customers from the old to the new location, Bill Browning felt that business, especially from Windsor, was adversely affected. The move, along with an economic recession, negative publicity from the accidents, the unpredictability of the *City of Wyandotte,* and the absence of new blockbuster rides to complement the roller coaster and log flume, contributed to a decline in attendance in 1975 to below six hundred thousand.[50]

The Brownings were at a crossroads in the amusement park game. Cedar Point was emerging as a megapark and rolling out new thrill rides and other attractions every year to overcome the economic doldrums and keep their turnstiles clicking, while Bob-lo struggled to break even. Thus it was necessary for the Brownings, even in difficult times, to keep the Bob-lo name in the news for positive reasons. In late August, they announced plans for a cable car that would transport

A brochure from the early 1970s employs
a slogan from the 1920s. Courtesy Dossin
Great Lakes Museum, Detroit, Michigan.

customers over the river from Amherstburg to Bob-lo. The plans also
called for the development of a new golf course and beach along with
a hotel.[51] But those plans never materialized.

In 1977 the old powerhouse was cleaned up and turned into a walk-
through fun house complete with black lights, a tilting floor, and a
rolling barrel at the exit. Attendance for the year was again below six
hundred thousand. Park hours were 11 AM until 8 PM and open to
midnight Saturdays. Admission for the boat ride alone was four dollars. One-price tickets, which included the boat fare and unlimited
rides, were eight dollars.[52] The company revived a Detroit steamboat
tradition when it sent the Columbia on a daylong trip through the St.
Clair Flats to Port Huron on a sweltering July 4. The ship was packed.

But changes in public perception of the city continued to challenge
the success of the Browning operation. The new dock at the foot of
Third was set apart from downtown and thus more vulnerable to se-

curity concerns related to youth gangs and the gang wars that were increasingly reported in the media. Moonlight charter organizers questioned whether there would be adequate police protection in the parking lots around the dock. Husbands thought twice about sending the wife and kids to the Detroit dock unescorted on a weekday. The Brownings believed that the combination of the new dock and the public's perception of security hurt their business.[53]

The company finally was forced to hire security staff for the boats, a job that had previously been handled by ship's crew. The Seafarers International Union had been notoriously slow to integrate, and the white deckhands simply could not respond to situations involving blacks on the boat without the risk of aggravating racial tensions. The only way to bypass the union was to engage a private security firm that could place their black officers on board, in essence adding to the cost of the transportation payroll.

On the island, management was concerned that some of the security staff were poorly trained and provided uneven treatment of patrons while handling situations. Malcontent employees fostered the impression that a majority of blacks among park patrons was resulting in an increase in security problems on an everyday basis. Yet park records showed that the only days when there may have been black majorities among the patronage were U.S. holidays, when the park was usually at capacity and there was a corresponding increase in the number of problems. Surveys also showed that black patrons spent more per capita than other parkgoers and generally were more appreciative of their overall park experience.[54] Bill Browning felt that, more than anything, it was the fear of blacks, not actual incidents, that caused a decline in attendance.

As part of their ongoing effort to maintain Bob-lo as a family friendly destination, the Brownings, like Walter Campbell before them, adopted several policies to keep the rowdyish elements off the boats and island. As in Campbell's era, changing times forced them to periodically revisit and revise those policies, a delicate balancing act faced by many in the entertainment industry.

For example, to prevent fights between rival motorcycle gangs, the Brownings maintained strict prohibition against the wearing of club insignias or colors. One evening, a black motorcycle club arrived in full regalia to attend a fundraiser for Detroit Common Council president Erma Henderson. After some deliberation, Ralph Browning allowed the group to board but without their jackets.

In the mid-1970s a coalition of groups sponsored Gay Pride Night on one of the moonlights. To counter public concerns of potential offensive behavior, Browning requested the groups to appoint marshals to act as chaperones. The night proved successful for both the local gay community and the company.

To avoid confrontation by students from rival schools, the Brownings were careful to consult with both police and school officials as they scheduled spring field trips to the park.

The company continued to place a U.S. immigration officer on the island to address concerns regarding people using the island as a way to get into the States from Canada. But the customs officer only came on duty in the afternoon, so passengers had to wait until four o'clock to board the first passenger boat back to Detroit. The company had to deal with two federal governments, a state and provincial government, several city governments, five unions for the boats alone, the Royal Canadian Mounted Police, the Environmental Protection Agency, the Coast Guard, and police and customs from both countries. Every municipality the boats ran through could cite them for any number of violations on the water. The Coast Guard mandated three engineers on the boats, when only two were really needed. The large ships, being registered in the United States, could not go from one Canadian port to another without going back to the United States first. Looking back, Bill Browning says:

> Between the race situation, labor, accidents, the operation of the boats, government issues and the media, I'm amazed that we were able to keep Bob-lo going as long as we did. The move of the docks to Third Street took away our prime location for people coming from Windsor on the tunnel bus. We had a financial loan being called in by a bank when the cost of a new ride could make the difference between a net profit or loss for the year. And the management team was all getting up in years. But it was the deterioration of the social climate—more gangs trying to come on the boat—that was one of the big factors in our decision to sell the operation. That environment took away Bob-lo's reputation of being a family park, someplace a husband, wife, and the kids could go to have a safe, fun day out.[55]

By contrast, Cedar Point, having solved their transportation problems by building a causeway for auto access, attracted three to four times the amount of customers as Bob-lo did, enabling it to invest $37 million back into their operation from the decade 1969–79. Since their peak year in 1974, the Bob-lo Company, without capital to put back into the operation, was presiding over attendance figures that were stagnating in the mid-five-hundred-thousand range. But in spite of those difficulties—most unseen by the public—Bob-lo remained a traditional place for families and groups to go. The St. Andrews Society, for one, continued to hold the Annual Highland Games at Bob-lo, as mentioned in "On the Bonnie Banks of Bob-lo," an item from the August 8, 1977, *Windsor Star:*

> One thousand pipers played at Bob-lo Island on Saturday. It was a sight to warm the heart of any Scotsman. . . . According to organizers of the 128th Highland gathering, more than 14,000 people attended despite poor weather. . . . This year's highland gathering was the largest ever for the Detroit Windsor area. Sponsored by the St. Andrew Society of Detroit, it attracted a record number of people.[56]

Midway through the 1978 season, the Skystreak coaster stopped at the top of a hill and rolled back down, injuring ten passengers.[57] Perhaps this was the proverbial straw that broke the camel's back. When it became difficult for the company to meet even its off-season payroll that winter, the Brownings quietly put the park up for sale.

Bob-lo in the mid-1970s heyday of the Brownings. Courtesy Dossin Great Lakes Museum, Detroit, Michigan.

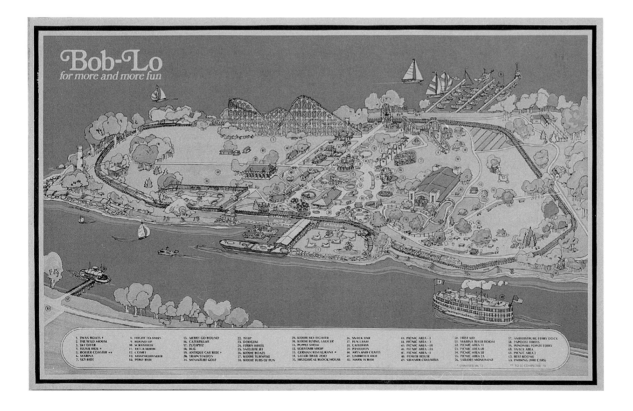

7

THRILLS AND SPILLS
IN THE AMUSEMENT
BUSINESS
1979–1993

New kids in town . . . An ominous beginning . . . The big boat problem . . . A year-round resort announced . . . Republicans do not nominate Bob-lo . . . Take someone you love . . . The debts are called in

It had been thirty years since Bob-lo was last up for sale. The Brownings' tenure had lasted from post–World War II to post-Vietnam, and they had managed to keep the park afloat when others had succumbed to the waves of change that swept the amusement park industry. Walled Lake had now been closed for almost a decade, and Edgewater Park was on its last legs. When the Brownings purchased Bob-lo in 1949, Disneyland was barely a gleam in its founder's eye; now Disneyland itself had been surpassed by Walt Disney World in Orlando. Bill Browning recalls, "I never lost faith in Bob-lo, but the investors were tired of losses and just wanted out. We looked for a buyer, but it was clear if we didn't get a buyer, we wouldn't have opened in 1979."[1]

Concerned that a collapse of Bob-lo could adversely affect plans to finance construction of Joe Louis Arena as well as cost hundreds of taxpayers' jobs, the city of Detroit requested that the Detroit Economic Growth Corporation evaluate marketing possibilities to help make the operation profitable. They concluded that better maintenance and more attractions would restore the patronage Bob-lo had before the recession of 1973–74, from which it had not recovered. While Bob-lo had shown a consistent profit, the company's debt prevented financing for large capital improvements. The assessment, however, was so positive that new investors were found almost immediately.[2]

In April 1979, weeks before the start of the new season, *Billboard Magazine* headlined, "Bob-lo Sold, Owners Eye Its Evolution." The new owners, a consortium of seven businessmen led by Billy Simpson of Kentucky and Rick Langlais of Minnesota, purchased the entire operation from the Brownings for an undisclosed amount estimated to be in the $5 million range, much of that amount in promissory notes and assumption of debts. Like their predecessors, the new owners had no previous experience in the amusement park field. Langlais stated that he was hesitant to invest because of the amount of "deferred maintenance" on the island but was convinced by Simpson, whom he had met when both were in an alcohol treatment center in Minnesota. They agreed to keep Bill Browning on as general manager for the 1979 season.[3]

The Brownings' corporate entities were consolidated into Cambridge Properties Incorporated, and the operation was renamed the Island of Bob-lo Company. Simpson and Langlais predicted that they would turn Bob-lo into a "Disneyland of the north" and that "fifteen years from now, people will be coming to Bob-lo instead of Cedar Point." Addressing the immediate future, Simpson acknowledged that Bob-lo would be a management challenge: "Bob-lo is extremely expensive to operate. It cost 45 percent of gross revenues last year just to operate the passenger boats." He stated that the new owners would concentrate on improving Bob-lo's eighteen-mile boat ride.[4] While Simpson may have been making perfect economic sense, his remarks were interpreted by many Bob-lophiles and ship lovers in the Detroit area as a threat to the continued operation of the beloved *Columbia* and *Ste. Claire,* inseparable in their minds from the Detroit riverfront and Bob-lo Island itself. Wary Detroiters perceived this as a lack of understanding and sensitivity, which fed concerns as to how these out-of-town owners might treat what most Detroit, Windsor, and Amherstburg residents thought of as "their" Bob-lo.

After a first season of operation that drew a disappointing five hundred thousand visitors, the company unveiled a five-year plan in a promotional news release in May 1980. On stationary headed "Bob-lo Island Amusement Park," the news release provided a brief history of the island and of the *Columbia* and the *Ste. Claire,* recognizing that both of the classic ships had been declared historic monuments by the U.S Department of the Interior. The company planned to refurbish both vessels in keeping with their five-year program. On the island, five new rides would be added to the park, including the Galaxy Enterprise, the Pirate Ship, the Polyp, Monster, and a new dodgems, although the old ride would continue to operate as well in its original stone building. The roller rink was converted to a thirteen-hundred-seat theater, where a daily live musical review would be performed. Also announced were plans for a renovated dock and restrooms, a new coaster, and a new craft village. The owners cancelled concession contracts that produced little profit and reorganized the island to run the restaurants, shops, rides, and other attractions themselves. They brought back respected former park engineer Gord Bacon, who personally inspected every ride and had critical components X-rayed for safety over the winter.

Perhaps the most intriguing component of the announced plan was the long-term goal to develop a resort complex, complete with hotel, golf course, and marina on the island: "This is in keeping with Bob-lo's plans to make the island a year-round amusement and resort center. The project will include using Bob-lo as a resort and conference center. When this dream is realized, a barge will be bought to transport guest cars through the winter."[5] But there would be a cost: the newly instituted pay-one-price ticket from Detroit would rise from \$9.75 to \$12.50 (with prices \$3 less from Amherstburg), and groups would no longer receive discounts. Fees for charters would more than double from \$2,000 to \$4,500.[6] The company's message was clear: with fixed costs of operating the boats at \$1,000 per hour, there was no longer any such thing as a free boat ride with Bob-lo.

Prior to the start of the 1980 season, the company hired Bob Garrison, a Six Flags veteran, to serve as general manager. But Garrison, with no experience in rebuilding amusement parks, immediately got off on the wrong foot with the Detroit market. Detroiters, accustomed to a more timely marketing approach as the weather actually got warmer, were perplexed at seeing Bob-lo heavily promoted in newspaper and television ads in late March. By the time the prolonged spring rains finally subsided in early June, the ad budget had been spent. Thus, while the owners may have been mystified to discover that only three people were on the first Bob-lo boat to the island for the season, Detroiters merely looked at the price, yawned, and waited for the real Bob-lo to open.

To add insult to injury, just as the weather and attendance began to improve, the Republican National Convention arrived in Detroit. But the long-expected shot in the arm from the champions of free enterprise never materialized for the Bob-lo owners. The boat docks' proximity to convention headquarters at Joe Louis Arena was declared a security threat. The Secret Service shut down the dock to all except delegates for the entire week of the convention. Bob-lo's attendance for the week fell from 32,000 the previous year to 786, with those customers coming through Amherstburg.

The *Ste. Claire* was reserved for evening dinner shows for the convention delegates. Phyllis Diller was booked for four nights, and Buddy Rich for two. Diller cancelled when only a handful of reservations came in. Rich played to fifteen people over his two-night stand. The *Columbia*, set aside for Republican charter cruises, sat idle when none were booked.

In an effort to bounce back, prices were lowered in mid-July, and the owners fired Garrison at the end of the month. Big band moonlights featuring Lionel Hampton, Count Basie, Woody Herman, Mercer Ellington, and Joe Vitale as well as concerts held as part of the Detroit

Mayor Coleman Young on the
SS Detroit (Columbia).
Photograph courtesy
Walter P. Reuther Library, Wayne State
University, Detroit, Michigan.

Montreaux Jazz Festival helped salvage the season. However, when the curtain came down, overall attendance was down to 270,000, reminiscent of Depression-era levels. Cash flow problems forced the owners to run the organization on a payroll-to-payroll basis, and they were forced to lay off all but five employees at the end of the year.[7] In assessing the debacle, the park public relations director acknowledged:

> We went in and tried to slug it out with Cedar Point and other big parks before we had the product. . . . We had the park's old image problem of being a park on the decline physically to overcome. We installed all the new rides and marketed ourselves as an alternative to Cedar Point. The mistake was, of the equipment we installed, nothing was really special and unique to Bob-lo . . . it was all something people had seen at Cedar Point. That coupled with the steep pay-one-price, turned people off. We also feel that people may have reacted to outsiders buying the park from a longstanding local family.[8]

By April 1981, reeling from 1980 losses of $3.5 million, the Island of Bob-lo Company was forced to declare bankruptcy. The Detroit Economic Growth Corporation, led by Al Schaffer, helped pull together a coalition of investors including Manufacturers National Bank and the National Bank of Detroit to bail them out. The Canadian Imperial Bank also bankrolled a significant portion of the bailout to assure payment to Canadian creditors. Fortunately, weeks before the island's scheduled opening date, the Canadian courts allowed the owners to open in spite of calls by creditors to liquidate.

Even given this respite, it looked at first like Bob-lo would once again fail to attract enough customers to survive. With no budget for a timely promotional campaign, attendance in the first month was under 100,000, with many weekend days drawing only 500 visitors. But then Schaffer volunteered his own nights and weekends to help management climb out of the hole they were in. He assisted in developing the television ad that featured the new theme "Take Someone You Love to Bob-lo," which was ready to run in July. By that point, the company was so cash-strapped that they had to literally run cash receipts from the ticket office to the television stations, which demanded payment before they would run the ad. Shaffer also solicited the advice of recently retired *Detroit Free Press* associate editor Frank Angelo, who convinced the management to stop treating the operation like Cincinnati's land-based King's Island and to focus on giving Detroiters the Bob-lo they wanted and would support. As a result, options were created to allow patrons to buy separate tickets for the boat ride and other island attractions and group sales discounts were reinstated. Angelo contacted the president of Farmer Jack, who agreed to a special two-for-one promotion through Farmer Jack stores. As a result, attendance turned around almost immediately and increased from 270,000 in 1980 to 450,000 in 1981 and helped the company finish $1 million in the black.[9]

In March 1982, the owners hired Schaffer as president, and he brought in Angelo as his vice president for marketing. Schaffer declared, "The latest big success story in Detroit is Bob-lo Island." Although anticipating another call for liquidation by the Canadian creditors, he expressed confidence that a new round of loans would help pay them off in full within two months and that the U.S. creditors would receive their due by the end of the year.[10]

No new rides were planned, and, in fact, upgrades of shows in the theater were the only improvements announced. Group sales and moonlight charters were up from 1981, with the big bands on Friday nights touted as weekly sellouts. The *Papoose V*—rechristened as the *Friendship on the River*—provided charter cruises for small groups out of the Detroit dock. Park hours were from 11 AM to 8:30 PM Monday through Friday and to 10:30 PM Saturday and Sunday. With a survey showing that the average customer spent $15 on the island in 1981, several combination ticket packages were offered. A complete package

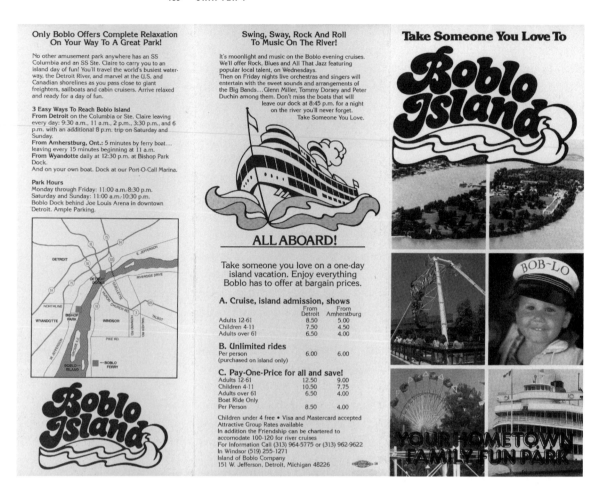

A 1982 brochure. Courtesy Dossin Great Lakes Museum, Detroit, Michigan.

including boat transportation, rides, and entertainment was $12.50 from Detroit and $9 from Amherstburg. Schaffer was confident that they would reach their goal of 750,000 visitors through an improved marketing strategy that targeted the 6 million potential customers in the Detroit and Windsor area.

As the season drew to a close, an old nemesis reared its head: the *Detroit News* headline "Bob-lo Alien-Smuggling Ring Busted" announced a Labor Day bust by the U.S. Immigration and Naturalization Services that netted twelve illegals and several Americans assisting them. The process was simple; immigrants came to the island by way of the Amherstburg ferry and exchanged return tickets with individuals who had come from Detroit. The INS spokesperson pointed out that this and several other island busts over the summer targeted only a for-profit smuggling ring and that the island was routinely used by immigrants seeking to enter with family assistance. "When we catch them, we just send them back," he said.[11]

When the dust settled, the park succeeded in attracting only 550,000 visitors—an increase but well below projections. The Canadian Imperial Bank and Manufacturers Bank of Detroit both called for their loans equaling $2 million to be repaid by October 15. Schaffer, ever the optimist, said,

> We can handle the debt on a long-term basis even with our present levels of attendance. When we took over the park in 1979, it was a mudhole and $3.5 million in debt. We have made that up and are now ready to become profitable. We turned the park around completely in three years time, investing $5 million in restoration and new rides. No one gave us a chance when we took it over. If we could perform that well in bad economic times, how much better can we do when the economy is healthier? We are not asking for any special deals or arrangements. It is time for the financial community to say to Bob-lo we are viable and deserve a normal, everyday debt structure.[12]

But the banks did not see it that way, and the debt was called. In November it was reported that the Island of Bob-lo Company was holding quiet negotiations with an unnamed friendly buyer who wanted to continue operating the island under present management. The company owed $9 million to the banks and had a total of 716 creditors. A ledger submitted to bankruptcy court estimated Bob-lo's assets at $15.3 million, most of that in fixed assets, including the two large ships valued at $7 million. A lawyer representing Bob-lo said that the creditors' best chance of being repaid was that the park be allowed to continue operating. Another lawyer representing the unsecured creditors expressed a "positive" feeling about Bob-lo being opened in the spring. The Canadian Imperial Bank, controller of the island, ensured that the park and rides were cared for over the winter. The U.S. bankruptcy judge George Brody set a January 15 date for bids to buy Bob-lo's assets with an auction date of January 31, 1983.[13]

In January, a flyer advertising the sale of the assets of Bob-lo Amusement Park was circulated by Price Waterhouse Ltd., Windsor. It listed the parcels available for sale as follows:

Parcel 1 That portion of Bois Blanc Island registered in the name of Bob-lo comprising approximately 272 acres.

Parcel 2 The lands in the town of Amherstburg and in the township of Malden registering in the name of Bob-lo comprising approximately 92 acres.

Parcel 3 The machinery, equipment, vehicles and amusement rides owned by Bob-lo set out in the terms and conditions of sale.

Parcel 4 Registered Canadian ships known as *Windmill Point, H E Gorry, Papoose III, Papoose IV* and *D&W Barge.*

Parcel 5 registered US vessels known as *Columbia* and *Ste. Claire.*

The flyer also listed thirty-three rides and the mini golf course along with their hourly ride capacities, ranging from the Pirate Ship and Sky-streak at 1,800 people per hour to the Satellite Jets and Flight to Mars at 250 people per hour.[14] There was no mention of the *Papoose V.*

DRIVING MISS BOB-LO, 1983–1988

An auction . . . AAA to the rescue . . . An investment . . . A new park and a new way to get there . . . Bob-lo blooms again . . . The carousel renewed . . . The Nightmare welcomed to the dance hall

As old man winter descended, blowing his icy breath over the island, the bidding began. Bankruptcy Judge Brody twice postponed his deadline for bids to allow various groups further time to develop their proposals. There appeared to be several interested groups of investors, but by late February only one group, led by one of the previous owners, had put down $500,000 on a bid. Their proposal was complicated by the fact that they were Canadian and, without an American partner, prohibited by U.S. maritime law from operating the U.S. registered steamers from Michigan ports to the Canadian island.[15] Elias Brothers Restaurants had also proposed a $5 million conditional offer, and the Seafarers International Union indicated interest primarily because they were owed $290,000, had first lien against one of the ships, and were interested in saving crew member jobs on the ship; but neither bid made it to the table.[16]

Just when it appeared that the judge would proceed with a ruling to liquidate, the *Windsor Star* reported that a proposal by the Automobile Club of Michigan (AAA) had been accepted and was given the right to assume management of the island until the sale was confirmed in late April 1983.[17]

AAA had been interested in the acquisition since they were approached for help in refinancing by the previous owners the past summer. Michael Wild, AAA spokesman, said of his company's interest,

"The idea grew out of a plan to look at our investments in a broader way than we had in the past. . . . [W]ith Bob-lo, we feel our return can be greater than through traditional investments."[18] Although AAA found the previous owners reluctant to cooperate with their refinancing proposal at that time, their interest was piqued. But when the island went up for bid in January, the AAA board balked because of lack of information. Had it not been for the court granted extensions, Bob-lo could easily have been liquidated.

The Canadian investors challenged the AAA offer, arguing that they made a legitimate offer of $7.5 million for the business. However, they did not post the $3.2 million security deposit as the court had ordered. The court approved the purchase for $6.5 million in late April, and AAA executives, Windsor mayor Elizabeth Kishkon, and Detroit mayor Coleman A. Young smiled from a dais celebrating the fact that Bob-lo had been saved. Wild issued a statement assuring that AAA had rehired most of the staff and were gearing up for a Memorial Day weekend opening. They planned no major changes and would concentrate on sprucing up the park for the coming season, hoping at least to match the paid attendance from 1982. Commenting on financing, Wild noted, "One positive factor we can bring to Bob-lo is a secure financial base. The park's biggest problem in the past was its need for short-term cash flow. The previous owners had to borrow money in order to improve the park and, when bad weather or a depressed economy cut into short term profits, they were unable to pay off the debt. AAA has the assets to weather market fluctuations. That is the biggest advantage we have."[19] AAA also had a tremendous built-in marketing advantage through their membership and offices located throughout the state.

On the issue of transportation, Wild offered a hint into the thinking that had already taken place: "Long term, we are studying alternative transportation to the island. Presently there are the large pleasure boats that transport patrons from Detroit and the ferry service on the Canadian side. We are looking at developing additional landing sites for the boats to make the transit easier." AAA raised the admission forty-five cents to $12.95 from Detroit and $8.95 from Canada. Wild lauded the efforts of the previous owners, noting their upgrades, new rides, and maintenance of the physical plant.[20]

By December, with the first season successfully behind them and Bob-lo attendance in the 520,000 range, AAA held a news conference at the Ponchartrain Hotel to announce $2.3 million dollars in improvements for the coming year. AAA president Jack Avignone said, "Changes are comprehensive, they address all age groups and a wide range of interests. The new Bob-lo will be a blend of tradition and technology which will appeal to the whole family. When complete, the entire park will have a turn of the century theme." A new children's play area would be designed to "challenge youngsters to use both their minds and muscles while having fun."[21]

In a nod to the past, AAA management brought in former owner Bill Browning as a consultant. Thirty resident tradesmen on the island had already relocated six rides along part of a new loop design of the park layout, and $500,000 went to upgrade the island's food service equipment, described by Wild as "antiquated." Picnic areas were improved. Entertainment was enhanced with a musical review in the Carousel Theater (the original carousel building and former roller rink) and a high dive show. Traveling entertainers and lively costumed characters were auditioned to roam the park. The highlight of the improvements was the addition of the Falling Star ride to be located near the dock. To encourage customer use of Amherstburg, a new season pass was offered. For $24.95, a patron could have unlimited admission to the park and its rides by way of Amherstburg. The pass was also good for one admission by way of the Detroit or Wyandotte docks.[22]

But perhaps the biggest changes in Bob-lo took place off the island. At Sault Ste. Marie two ships, the *Gibraltar* and *Tecumseh,* were built to service a new Bob-lo dock at Humbug Marina in Gibraltar. The ships were sixty-five feet long with a capacity of three hundred passengers each. The run to Bob-lo took forty-five minutes and allowed AAA to expand its market to Monroe and northern Ohio. The company credited

The Sky Streak (in the foreground).
Photograph courtesy Dossin Great Lakes
Museum, Detroit, Michigan.

much of their 5 percent increase in attendance for 1984 to this new operation.[23]

In February of 1985, Bob-lo announced the addition of a Vekoma Corkscrew roller coaster at a cost of $1.2 million. The coaster came in parts by ship from Belgium to Montreal and then by rail to Amherstburg. Additional improvements included a renovated miniature golf course and landscaping of Kiddieland. A gift shop was added at the rear of the island. Admission from Detroit increased to $13.95.[24]

In August 1985, the Detroit police received a call from the wife of a fired U.S. postal employee, who claimed her husband had planted a bomb aboard the *Columbia* in the hope of exploding his supervisor on his one-day fun day to Bob-lo. The police checked the ship for evidence of a bomb and found none. On board they found the postal supervisor, who said he had never even heard of the alleged bomber. The result was that the *Columbia* was delayed an hour and a half on her departure.[25]

In late November *Amusement Business* reported, "Record Year at Bob-lo." Bob-lo general manager Dan Aylward said, "This is the year that everything jelled," exulting in an attendance of 725,000 for the season. He attributed the increase to the new coaster and to expanded group sales, which were up 44 percent and accounted for 33 percent of total attendance. Aylward said the biggest challenge the park faced was that there were not enough boats to transport the patrons: "There were times we had to close the Detroit and Gibraltar docks and direct patrons to drive to Amherstburg."[26] Roughly two-thirds of patrons came from the two U.S. docks. Bob-lo widened its target audience from ages eighteen to thirty-four to ages eighteen to forty-nine and engaged in year-round marketing at trade shows. They even built a replica of the *Columbia* to be used as a float in the Thanksgiving Day and other parades. They bought outdoor advertising in areas more than one hundred miles away and ran heavy radio promotions with giveaways and revived remote broadcasts from the park. The live shows were well received, and the new merchandise building had difficulty keeping up stock to meet demand. While good weather contributed to the increase

The new boats at Gibraltar dock. Photograph courtesy Dossin Great Lakes Museum, Detroit, Michigan.

in attendance, the island did sustain three days of power outages resulting from lightning strikes on the mainland.

The 1986 season posted numbers almost as good as the previous year, with attendance just under seven hundred thousand. A new vessel, the 585-passenger Toledo-built *Lynwood Beattie* (named after the recently deceased captain of the *Columbia*), was added to the Gibraltar fleet, and the venerable ships *Columbia* and *Ste. Claire* competed in a riverboat race captained by WXYZ newscaster Bill Bonds and WJR disc jockey J. P. McCarthy. AAA also decided to reinvest in the first ride to ever grace the park—the carousel. Created by Russian-born artist Marcus Charles Illions, who emigrated to the United States in the 1880s, the carousel was considered one of the best of the 170 wooden carousels remaining in North America. More than just amusement rides, these carousels were regarded as folk art and were fetching up to $700,000 in recent auctions with individual pieces going for as much as $25,000. Each of the Bob-lo figures would cost $2,000 to restore.

Courtesy Dossin Great Lakes Museum, Detroit, Michigan.

The former powerhouse turned into a gift shop. Photograph courtesy Dossin Great Lakes Museum, Detroit, Michigan.

Atlantic West in Milan, Ohio, was selected for the work. Artistic director Tom Layton observed that carousels still paid for themselves slowly but surely because they did not break down or become obsolete like most thrill rides.[27] That year AAA invested in another ride destined to become a Bob-lo landmark—a 375-foot-tall tower that would transport over fifty people at a time to a bird's-eye view of the island, Lake Erie, and the entire downriver area with glimpses of the distant Detroit skyline. The tower came from a park in San Pedro, California, and was soon sporting the AAA logo at its peak.

The beginning of the 1987 season was marked by another reloca-
tion of the Detroit docks, this time almost two miles downriver to the
foot of Clark Street. Since the completion of the Joe Louis Arena several years earlier, it had been evident that the competition for parking spaces near the dock was becoming an issue. AAA accented the
positive, noting easy access to the Fisher Freeway and thousands of
dockside parking spots.

Although ticket prices increased to $15.95 from Detroit and $12.95
from Gibraltar and Amherstburg, Bob-lo moved smoothly through the
1987 season, announcing attendance figures again in the seven-hun-
dred-thousand range. Although the weather was rainier than normal,
fifty-three days above 85 degrees made Bob-lo an attractive destination
for city dwellers that summer. AAA expanded the park season to include every weekend in both May and September with service from its
Amherstburg and Gibraltar docks.

In August park management cooperated with the Ontario Provincial Police (OPP) to ensure that the sixth annual Bob-lo gathering of
the Outlaws Motorcycle Club did not have a chance to get out of hand.
OPP was waiting at the dock as the bikers disembarked at the island.

*The Columbia at the island in the 1980s.
Photograph courtesy Marsh Collection
Society, Amherstburg, Ontario.*

More than forty police and immigration authorities rode herd on the 125 bikeless club members, detaining 30 in a makeshift pen, arresting 4, and deporting 3 as undesirable aliens. One of the members, Duke, was quoted as saying, "We don't usually talk to the press, but we usually don't get jerked around this bad either. We didn't wear our colors or nothin', man. We're just here to have fun and this is the kind of thing they pull? Unbelievable. We paid $12.95 for this?"[28] General manager Dan Aylward responded that the park was simply allowing OPP and immigration to do its job and that AAA had nothing to do with the police operation.

The Gibraltar dock added a small boat to its fleet, and the Amherstburg dock operated its two *Papoose* ships. AAA had now owned the park for five years and had invested $12 million over that period. A new ride—the Nightmare—was set to be unveiled for the coming year. It would be an indoor dark coaster built into the floor of the western half of the dance hall. The eastern half of the long vacant hall had already been converted by AAA into an international-themed pavilion.[29]

Follies in Nightmare Town, 1988–1992

A shock and a rude awakening . . . Out-of-towners regain the helm . . . Rowdies breach the gates . . . Good-bye, carousel . . . Good-bye, *Columbia* and *Ste. Claire* . . . Divesting without care

Another shock greeted Detroiters the following spring: "We would not have sold Bob-lo if we had not achieved our two objectives: to preserve and restore it," said Larry Givens, AAA spokesperson. "There was no conscious decision made by us; had we not been approached, I think we would still have Bob-lo Island."[30] And, just like that, Detroiters learned that Bob-lo had been sold again, this time to International Broadcasting Corporation (IBC) for the reported sum of $21 million. IBC bought an operation that AAA had driven out of debt and into a fiscally solvent operation with no debt and record-high attendance levels. The park was estimated to generate about $17 million in annual income at the time of sale.

The IBC chief executive officer, Thomas Scallen, explained that his company was trying to strengthen their summer season holdings through the purchase. IBC also owned the Ice Capades, the Harlem Globetrotters, and a film production company. Since the transaction would not be completed until June 1, IBC benefited further from the

$2.6 million that AAA invested in the operation over the winter, including the addition of a band organ to the carousel, relocation of some rides, the new Nightmare, ethnic restaurants in the International Pavilion, and expanded parking and lighting at the Detroit Clark Street docks. The theater in the old roller rink was converted to Mark Wilson's Haunted Theater, and Captain Andy's Rivertown Review, featuring fourteen animated characters, performed in another 350-seat theater.[31] But before the deal was even closed, the island and boats experienced a Memorial Day to remember on May 30, 1988.

Hints of trouble had surfaced earlier in the day when Bob-lo company officials on the Canadian island called upon the OPP to quell sporadic fighting among the ten thousand fun seekers on the island. About thirty OPP officers—with cruisers and a paddy wagon—were taken to the island by barge at about 4 PM to reinforce two OPP officers and Bob-lo's resident security staff. The officers, wearing bullet proof vests, patrolled the island until after the last boats were loaded for Detroit that evening.

The rowdiness continued on the steamers returning to the city. The *Columbia*'s twenty security guards were unable to control sporadic fighting that caused panic stricken passengers to surge from one side of the ship to the other. The captain, concerned that his ship was listing dangerously, placed a distress call to which the Coast Guard responded. The *Columbia* made it to the dock safely but was listing too severely on the port side to allow the gangplank to be lowered. People began jumping to the dock from the second deck, and the fighting spilled over onto the dock, where a contingent of Detroit police tried to intervene. The Coast Guard boat stood by the *Columbia* to make sure no one had gone into the water and to await the *Ste. Claire* coming into Detroit with a similar load of trouble.[32]

With headlines that screamed, "Mayday on the Bob-lo Boats," things were not exactly starting off on the right foot for Scallen and IBC. Although they managed to get through the rest of the season without further mishap, the public was acutely aware that the "rowdy elements" that Walter Campbell had warned against so many decades before had breached the gates. Surprisingly, attendance for the season was not significantly affected by the incident, perhaps because of all the positive publicity that had been generated by AAA over the previous years and because group picnics had already been booked.

The 1989 season began on May 6 with the park open weekends from 11 AM to 8:30 PM. From May 23 to June 9, the park offered special weekday hours from 11 AM to 5:30 PM to accommodate school groups. The rest of the summer the park was open until 10:30 on weekends and 8:30 on weekdays. After Labor Day, the park again ran on the weekends through the end of September. New for the year was a Chinese acrobat troupe and the Ski Fever Spectacular, performed off the west side of the island. A clown band patrolled the midway.

> Hurtling, twisting, rolling, dipping, spinning, soaring, bumping, plummeting, leaping—or just moseying along—our rides have all the right moves for every mood and age.
>
> Daredevils will meet their match on coasters like the Screamer Corkscrew, the Sky Streak, and that ultimate horror trip, the Nightmare.
>
> For fun without fright, there are such ever popular standbys as the Giant Ferris Wheel, the Antique Carrousel, the wildly refreshing Log Flume and the chug-a-lug Miniature Train.
>
> You can reach new heights from the Falling Star, or the rotating perch of the Sky Tower.
>
> And, if you like to take a change in the fast lane, Bumper Cars provide all the motion and commotion you could ask for.[33]

With a relatively peaceful season, attendance for 1989 was given as 597,000, once considered healthy for the operation but down 100,000 from AAA's last year in 1987.

In February 1990 Scallen announced that the 1906 merry-go-round restored by AAA only a few years earlier would be auctioned off at the end of the month and that the auctioned figures would be replaced with fiberglass ones. "The kid doesn't care if they're wood or fiberglass, and they're too valuable to expose to the elements or to theft," said Scallen.[34] A few weeks later, *Amusement Business* announced that, since there were no bidders for the entire carousel for $985,000, the pieces had been sold separately. The sale netted over $860,000 and resulted in several records for the individual pieces, including $34,000 for the outside row deer. The Stinson reproduction band organ, new to the park in 1987, sold for $35,000.

For the 1990 season IBC tried to vary its marketing strategy and succeeded in increasing attendance to 609,000 in spite of rain during eleven of the nineteen weekends. Group sales accounted for 35 percent of total ticket sales. The pay-one-price ticket rose to $16.95 from Detroit, with a season ticket from Gibraltar or Amherstburg running $39.95, which accounted for seventy-five thousand of the tickets sold. The owners also instituted a new half-day ticket selling for $8.50

after three o'clock. For the first time, management closed the park to the general public for the Sunday and Monday of Labor Day weekend and rented it to Henry Ford Hospital for staff and family outings for those two days, drawing 22,000 people and essentially selling out the park. According to marketing director Tim Dagg, the two most popular rides that year were the train and the observation tower, with Mark Wilson's World's Greatest Illusions playing to a packed theater. Promised for the new year was a hands-on family show that would feature a wide assortment of animals. Negotiations for a new ride were also under way.[35]

By all accounts the 1991 season should have been declared a success. Attendance increased to 630,000, even though the park was open fewer days in May and September.[36] The Back to Bones show featured exotic animals, and characters from *The Simpsons* entertained in the midway near Fort Fun. An outdoor roller rink and roller blade rental area were opened, and a 1.5-mile bicycle path and bike rental were now available. The International Pavilion (formerly the dance hall) was once again converted—this time to an arcade and souvenir emporium, with gamers and shoppers unfazed by the screams emanating from the Nightmare coaster churning just on the other side of the wall. Pepsi signed on as corporate sponsor for the Log Flume, and Columbo Yogurt and Winter Sausage were designated the official yogurt and hot dogs of Bob-lo Island. The large boats had five departures a day from the Clark Street docks and six on weekends.[37] Management made these gains in spite of their unusual decision to close the park on Tuesdays. Their intent "to cut costs and to give employees a day off" was unprecedented in Bob-lo's history and signaled uncertainty to Bob-lo watchers in the community. At this point, the park had two hundred year-round and six hundred seasonal employees and paid $270,000 a year to Malden Township in taxes.[38]

In spite of all these signs of success, when the 1991 season ended, IBC declared bankruptcy and among all its holdings offered only Bob-lo for sale. The asking price for the operation was $9 million, less than half of the purchase price from AAA. New CEO Jim Sullivan said of the drastic price reduction, "We paid too much for it." IBC sold the *Columbia* and *Ste. Claire* for $235,000 in October, eliminating the annual operating cost of $2.4 million for the ships.[39] The high costs of operating the steamers had been an issue for every management group since the Ferry Company went out of business in the late 1930s, but it was almost inconceivable to Detroiters that the ships would actually ever be pulled from service while still in good operating condition. With the ships out of commission and the Detroit docks closed, the vast ma-

In author's collection.

jority of park goers would be faced with a new travel decision the next summer: Amherstburg or Gibraltar.

Even with the company in bankruptcy, Sullivan made the decision to go ahead with the 1992 season. He believed the park could be profitable and invested an additional $2 million in renovations and start-up costs, including a major renovation of the dance hall building. In regard to the transportation situation, Sullivan said, "We have worked out the logistics. We have all the boat power we need, but we need most people to come to the park from Canada. We can handle a million if they all come from the Canadian side."[40]

Sullivan predicted that IBC would be out of bankruptcy by June.[41] However, in May with the opening weeks away, projected attendance for Bob-lo was downsized to four hundred thousand, reflecting the fact that the large boats would not be running from Detroit.[42] The new advertising slogan was "The One Day Funday for the Whole Family!" and the park advertised a new children's petting zoo and Kids Kingdom redesigned from Fort Fun. The park was again open seven days a week from 10 AM until 9 PM after the Fourth of July. This led to the conjecture that the previous year's Tuesday closings were related more to cutting costs on the steamers than any other single thing.

1993, the last year of the park. Courtesy Dossin Great Lakes Museum, Detroit, Michigan.

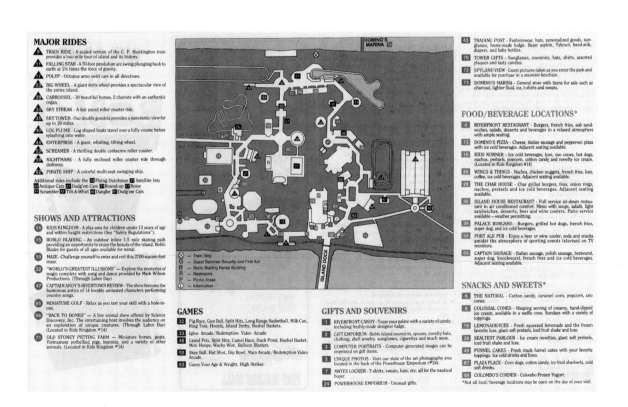

MAJOR RIDES

A TRAIN RIDE - A scaled version of the C. P. Huntington train provides a two-mile tour of island and its history.

11 FALLING STAR - A 70-foot pendulum arc swing plunging back to earth at 2½ times the force of gravity.

17 POLYP - Octopus arms swirl cars in all directions.

B BIG WHEEL - A giant ferris wheel provides a spectacular view of the entire island.

29 CARROUSEL - 30 beautiful horses, 2 chariots with an authentic organ.

34 SKY STREAK - A fast paced roller coaster ride.

35 SKY TOWER - Our double gondola provides a panoramic view for up to 20 miles.

40 LOG FLUME - Log shaped boats travel over a hilly course before splashing into water.

41 ENTERPRISE - A giant, whirling, tilting wheel.

53 SCREAMER - A thrilling double corkscrew roller coaster.

56 NIGHTMARE - A fully enclosed roller coaster ride through darkness.

62 PIRATE SHIP - A colorful multi-seat swinging ship.

Additional rides include the **12** Flying Dutchman **21** Satellite Jets **23** Antique Cars **27** Dodg'em Cars **51** Round-up **57** Rotor **61** Scrambler **42** Tilt-A-Whirl **60** Dangler **65** Dodg'em Cars

SHOWS AND ATTRACTIONS

14 KIDS KINGDOM - A play area for children under 12 years of age and within height restrictions (See "Safety Regulations").

15 BOBLO BLADING - An outdoor inline 1.5 mile skating path providing an opportunity to enjoy the beauty of the island. Boblo Blades for guests of all ages available for rental.

19 MAZE - Challenge yourself to enter and exit this 2700-square-foot maze.

22 "WORLD'S GREATEST ILLUSIONS" — Explore the mysteries of magic complete with song and dance provided by Mark Wilson Productions. (Through Labor Day)

47 CAPTAIN ANDY'S RIVERTOWN REVIEW - The show features the humorous antics of 14 animated characters performing country songs.

55 MINIATURE GOLF - Relax as you test your skill with a hole-in-one.

66 "BACK TO BONES" — A live animal show offered by Science Discovery, Inc. The entertaining host involves the audience on an exploration of unique creatures. (Through Labor Day) (Located in Kids Kingdom #14)

71 OLD STONEY PETTING FARM — Miniature horses, goats, Vietnamese potbellied pigs, bunnies, and a variety of other animals. (Located in Kids Kingdom #14)

Train Stop
G — Guest Services/Security and First Aid
B — Boblo Blading Rental Building
R — Restrooms
P — Picnic Areas
I — Information

GAMES

32 Pig Race, Gun Ball, Split Hits, Long Range Basketball, Milk Can, Ring Toss, Hoopla, Island Derby, Bushel Baskets.

33 Igloo Arcade/Redemption Video Arcade

46 Grand Prix, Split Hits, Camel Race, Duck Pond, Bushel Basket, Mini Hoops, Wacky Wire, Balloon Blasters.

52 Skee Ball, Hot Shot, Dip Bowl, Main Arcade/Redemption Video Arcade.

63 Guess Your Age & Weight, High Striker.

GIFTS AND SOUVENIRS

1 RIVERFRONT CANDY - Tease your palate with a variety of candy, including freshly-made designer fudge.

2 GIFT EMPORIUM - Boblo Island souvenirs, spoons, novelty hats, clothing, shell jewelry, sunglasses, cigarettes and much more.

3 COMPUTER PORTRAITS - Computer generated images can be imprinted on gift items.

5 UNIQUE PHOTOS - Visit our state of the art photography area located in the back of the Powerhouse Emporium (#24).

7 MATES LOCKER - T-shirts, sweats, hats, etc. all for the nautical buyer.

24 POWERHOUSE EMPORIUM - Unusual gifts.

43 TRADING POST - Fashionwear, hats, personalized goods, sunglasses, home-made fudge, Bayer aspirin, Tylenol, band-aids, diapers, and baby bottles.

70 TOWER GIFTS - Sunglasses, souvenirs, hats, shirts, assorted plaques and tasty candies.

72 SPYLAND VIEW - Guest pictures taken as you enter the park and available for purchase in a souvenir keychain.

73 DOMINO'S MARINA - General store with items for sale such as charcoal, lighter fluid, ice, t-shirts and sweats.

FOOD/BEVERAGE LOCATIONS*

4 RIVERFRONT RESTAURANT - Burgers, french fries, sub sandwiches, salads, desserts and beverages in a relaxed atmosphere with ample seating.

13 DOMINO'S PIZZA - Cheese, italian sausage and pepperoni pizza with ice cold beverages. Adjacent seating available.

18 KIDS KORNER - Ice cold beverages, Icee, sno cones, hot dogs, nachos, pretzels, popcorn, cotton candy and novelty ice cream. (Located in Kids Kingdom #14)

20 WINGS & THINGS - Nachos, chicken nuggets, french fries, Icee, coffee, ice cold beverages. Adjacent seating available.

28 THE CHAR HOUSE - Char grilled burgers, fries, onion rings, nachos, pretzels and ice cold beverages. Adjacent seating available.

30 ISLAND HOUSE RESTAURANT - Full service sit-down restaurant in air conditioned comfort. Menu with soups, salads, light sandwiches, desserts, beer and wine coolers. Patio service available – weather permitting.

39 PALACE BURGERS - Burgers, grilled hot dogs, french fries, super dog, and ice cold beverages.

54 PORT ALE PUB - Enjoy a beer or wine cooler, soda and snacks amidst the atmosphere of sporting events televised on TV monitors.

64 CAPTAIN SAUSAGE - Italian sausage, polish sausage, bratwurst, super dog, knockwurst, french fries and ice cold beverages. Adjacent seating available.

SNACKS AND SWEETS*

6 THE NATURAL - Cotton candy, caramel corn, popcorn, sno cones.

9 COLOSSAL CONES - Heaping serving of creamy, hand-dipped ice cream, available in a waffle cone. Sundaes with a variety of toppings.

10 LEMONADE/ICEE - Fresh squeezed lemonade and the frozen favorite Icee, giant soft pretzels, iced fruit shake and Icee.

38 SEALTEST PARLOUR - Ice cream novelties, giant soft pretzels, iced fruit shake and Icee.

49 FUNNEL CAKES - Fresh made funnel cakes with your favorite toppings. Ice cold drinks and Icees.

67 PLAZA PLACE - Corn dogs, cotton candy, icy fruit sherberts, cold soft drinks.

68 COLOMBO'S CORNER - Colombo Frozen Yogurt.

*Not all food/beverage locations may be open on the day of your visit.

Fun Is Just a Short Boat Ride Away!

No Need to drive for hours or spend a lot of money to have fun.
Bob-lo is conveniently located on a Canadian island in the Detroit River—just a short boat ride from both the Canadian and
Michigan shorelines. With such easy access, you'll have more
time to enjoy Bob-lo's many attractions.[43]

In fact, the reality was much worse. The big boats had been indel-
ibly linked to the existence of the island park in the minds of too many
Metro Detroiters who could not imagine Bob-lo without the *Ste. Claire*
and *Columbia*. Faced with the choice of Amherstburg or Gibraltar,
people stayed away in droves. Bob-lo drew only three hundred thousand in 1992, less than half of the previous year's attendance and the
lowest figure since the disastrous 1980 season.[44]

THE LAST RIDE, 1993

**Another auction . . . The new new kids . . . A glorious Fourth . . . Hope for the future
. . . The tragedy of liquidation**

With no takers at IBC's selling price, the park and its assets were
again put on the court-ordered auction block as a single entity. One
successful bidder could take over the entire operation and again save
the park from piecemeal liquidation. To qualify for bidding, a deposit of $250,000 was required. Auctioneer David Norton of Coldwater
estimated the Bob-lo operation would sell for anywhere between $2
million and $8 million. The bankruptcy court set the auction date in
February to allow a new owner time to prepare the park for the 1993
season. The auction was held at the Marriott at Detroit Metro Airport
so that weather would not interfere with bidders' travel. There were
seven bidders for Bob-lo, the largest amusement park ever auctioned
in the United States; the highest bid—$3.8 million—was not accepted
due to failure to comply with financial obligations as stipulated by the
court.[45]

By February 10 Bob-lo had new owners—Michael Moodenbaugh
and Jeff Stock, two young Seattle entrepreneurs who had experienced
success with real estate and Enchanted Parks, an amusement park
located between Seattle and Tacoma that they purchased two years
earlier. Lacking the $3.7 million needed to acquire Bob-lo, Mooden-
baugh approached the Seattle-based Beneroya family, known for their

local philanthropic efforts. The Beneroyas, also known for their con-servative business practices, agreed to back Moodenbaugh and Stock through their Northern Capital Company in a fifty-fifty partnership. The partnership was based on the understanding that all profits would be applied directly to the principal of the loan with profits after that time split fifty-fifty between Northern Capital and Omni Properties Ltd., Moodenbaugh and Stock's company. The two companies signed a contract that only went through September 15, 1993, as it was the Beneroyas' intent to closely scrutinize their investment in Mooden-baugh and Stock's venture. Included in the sale were thirty-one rides, thirty-five attractions, and all boats and buildings as well as the ninety-acre Amherstburg dock property.[46] The *Columbia* and *Ste. Claire,* pre-viously sold and now in the hands of the Detroit Economic Growth Corporation, were not included.

After the auction, Moodenbaugh, operating as the active partner while Stock stayed in Seattle to manage those holdings, announced that general manager David Brown and his staff would remain in place: "The team in place is very capable of operating and promoting a park . . . their hands had been tied and they had no tools to work with. They couldn't get operating capital from their parent company and, as a result, the park's market share fell, as did its reputation. We want to untie the hands of management and give them the tools they need to increase our market penetration." Addressing the still sensitive issue of island access, Moodenbaugh said, "If people want to come, we'll get them there. Getting the people to want to come is the major problem right now."[47] He knew that bringing the Detroit boat operation back was not a viable option and so concentrated on getting people to the island from the Amherstburg and Gibraltar docks. He initiated pro-motional events on the island and combination tickets that made it attractive for families to come to Bob-lo.

By late June, Moodenbaugh realized that his challenge to make Bob-lo profitable again would be a difficult one. He traded his interest in Omni Properties to Stock in exchange for Stock's share of Bob-lo and moved to Detroit so that he could focus on preparing for the 1994 season. On his to do list were selling sponsorships, organizational outings, expanding the marina, paving the Amherstburg parking lot, expanding the docks, putting in a major new ride—probably a coast-er—and starting to work on a waterslide park.

Something clicked. Moodenbaugh's first special events over the Fourth of July weekend included big-name musical acts and a giant fireworks display that helped set attendance records for both single

days and weekends on the island. On Saturday 17,812 people turned out, and so did another 16,945 on Sunday.[48] This was the first demonstration that enough patrons could be drawn from the Amherstburg dock without reliance on the Detroit boats.

The complexity of managing as vast an operation as Bob-lo—even without the large boats—caught up with Moodenbaugh. Although the July 4 weekend was an unqualified success attendance-wise, park employees felt that poor planning forced them to work almost around the clock. In mid-August Moodenbaugh threatened to close down the park if Canadian Coast Guard and immigration officials refused to allow the U.S. registered boats based in Gibraltar to ferry passengers directly from Amherstburg to the island, against regulations.[49]

A couple weeks later, there was a report that Moodenbaugh cut off water from the island's filtration plant to seventy-two-year-old Dorothy Tresness, who occupied the remaining private cottage on the island's western shore. Moodenbaugh claimed that the shutoff was forced by the island's insurance company. The move resulted in some embarrassing press for Moodenbaugh as area boaters dropped off hundreds of gallons of bottled water to the Tresness cottage and local media feasted on the story.[50]

As Labor Day arrived, some of the Moodenbaugh magic dissipated. Rainy weather brought only four thousand people to the island in spite of a free Beach Boys concert. By that point the island had attracted four hundred thousand customers for the year, an increase from 1992 but still below the break-even level. Plans were made to keep the island open every weekend through Halloween for the first time, and Moodenbaugh was able to extend his contract with Northern Capital to September 29, buying himself a couple of weeks to find a new investor. In mid-September, Moodenbaugh announced that Bob-lo would close its Gibraltar docks for the next season and move all ship operations to Amherstburg, where a new dock would be built to accommodate three ships at a time. He also announced that the corporate offices in Wyandotte would be closed and moved to the island itself. For the first time in its history, the amusement park would be run entirely from the Canadian side.[51] This meant that Moodenbaugh would be freed of the responsibilities of having to accommodate the laws and regulations of two governments both on the water and on the island. His ferries would no longer navigate in American waters, and the customs problem would now be handled at the border crossings. Moodenbaugh had cut the strings that had made Bob-lo such a complex undertaking for generations of previous owners. The fact that he did not have the large steamers and their sentimental value to contend with as he took over Bob-lo enabled him to see the operation from an entirely different perspective than the previous owners. Given the choice, most Detroiters preferred the drive to Amherstburg over the drive to the less familiar town of Gibraltar and the forty-five-minute boat ride to the island from Humbug Marina.

The first two weekends of September were designated as cheerleader weekends, with teams from schools throughout the area competing for prizes and bringing lots of family and relatives to the park. The following weekend featured a Crystal Gayle concert that was poorly attended. And then, on September 24, Moodenbaugh was critically injured when he flipped the Ford Bronco he was driving in Toledo. He was not expected to live. Within a few days of the accident, Beneroya

Courtesy Dossin Great Lakes Museum, Detroit, Michigan

family representatives arrived in Detroit and canceled events for the rest of the season and ordered staff to stop booking groups for the coming year. Within a week the locks on the Bob-lo offices had been changed and the park staff laid off. While the Beneroyas' representatives oversaw the park being put in mothballs for the winter, Moodenbaugh recovered enough to be moved home in December to a hospital near Seattle. He had no energy to think about Bob-lo, only enough to focus on recovering his health.[52]

As the new year rolled around, the severity of Moodenbaugh's injuries made it apparent that he would not be able to continue management of the park operation, and the Beneroyas decided to cut their losses. Bill Weisfield, chief operating officer for Northern Capital, said that the company had poured an additional $3 million into the island over the season and that it was time to stop the bleeding. Having received no interested buyers for the entire operation, they would not even entertain the winner-take-all-style auction through which Moodenbaugh acquired the island. The Beneroyas stipulated that the park's assets be sold piecemeal and the island and boats sold separately as well. Weisfield stated, "We have no debt from secured creditors. We want to do this right."[53] He went on to say that all 1,050 employees who worked at the park had been paid in full and all their benefits had been paid. All real estate taxes were up to date and all utility bills current. He estimated that they would need to realize $8.5 million on the sale to make everything whole. The auction listing price for all thirty rides came to $2.5 million, with the highest priced item being the Corkscrew coaster at $850,000. It was also possible to pick up the Kiddie Whip or a mini coaster for $4,000 each. The 315-foot Skytower was listed at $200,000 and the recently installed Nightmare at $350,000. All rides were FOB (free on board) Amherstburg, meaning that the sellers would dismantle the rides and convey them across the river for the buyer to pick up. Weisfield expressed hopes of selling the fleet of six ferry boats to the new casino in Windsor to transport gamblers across from Detroit. The island and parcels of land were appraised at $6 million, and the land was in the process of being rezoned from a strictly amusement park to an amusement park and residential zoning. This would allow a golf course–based cluster condominium complex that Weisfield thought would be "perfect" for the island.[54]

As the dismantling of Bob-lo proceeded, the hope of Detroiters and Amherstburgians began to fade. Moodenbaugh still entertained hopes of developing the park as a concert venue and creating special events to draw visitors. From his Seattle hospital bed, he said, "The day will come when I can battle like I used to and fight to take back Bob-lo."[55]

In author's collection.

Detroit mayor Dennis Archer said, "I hope whoever winds up with the island itself will put it to the kind of use which will be of benefit to Canada, where it's located, and will be a benefit to those of us who live in the metropolitan area and the city of Detroit." An Amherstburg developer said of the island, "There hasn't been too much talk about it. I imagine it could be attractive. I'm not sure whom it would be attractive to. Someone who has a lot of money could buy up the whole thing and put up quite an estate."[56] The land was to be sold except the properties held by Dorothy Tresness and the former Randall property, now owned by John and Diane Pandolfo, who had already constructed a beautiful year-round dwelling where Lookout Cottage once stood. The four acres once owned by Randall had been expanded to twenty-one acres with the inclusion of the water lots and Horseshoe Island off its tip.

For Moodenbaugh, the feuding with his ex-partner, Jeff Stock, and the Beneroyas' Northern Capital carried on in two lawsuits. After returning to Seattle in 1994, Moodenbaugh underwent lung surgery and years of rehabilitation for the paralysis that left him in a wheelchair. His wife of seventeen years then divorced him and, because Stock had canceled his health care insurance while he was still in a coma, he had to declare bankruptcy. In the first suit, Moodenbaugh was requesting Stock and Omni Properties to pay for his health bills and emotional stress caused by the cancellation since the accident. Moodenbaugh also contended that the Beneroyas sold Bob-lo against his will, and he was asking for compensation for their actions in selling the island and its assets. However, his attorneys advised him to accept an out of court settlement with Northern Capital, and he agreed. Moodenbaugh lamented, "If I could change anything, I'd change that management contract. And I would have looked harder for another investor. I shouldn't have taken their money in the first place."[57]

The Amusement Park Era: A Summary

Throughout its history as an amusement park, Bob-lo Island was distinguished by its unique location. The geographic setting of the island at the mouth of the Detroit River eighteen miles from the burgeoning city of Detroit made it an ideal site for the Detroit, Windsor, and Belle Isle Ferry Company seeking to diversify its operation by transporting patrons to a new recreation destination. The island's proximity to the city allowed the ferries to make full use of their passenger-carrying capacity, thus significantly enhancing the fleet's earning potential. Yet it was remote enough from the city that, by the last bend in the river, the smokestacks were out of sight and thoughts of the rat race were driven out of mind by visions of green, leafy trees and Lake Erie on the horizon. Throw in the fact that the Union Jack greeted passengers coming onto the island operated by natives of nearby Amherstburg, and the Detroit park goer enjoyed the added experience of being a visitor to a foreign land, if only for a day.

The combination of the growing Detroit auto industry and the emergence of a well-paid working class made a family outing to Bob-lo a possibility that evolved into a ritual for thousands of Detroit families every summer. The Ferry Company capitalized on that fact to build two large Detroit-based ships that would cater to that clientele for the better part of the century. The capacity of those ships, as well as the prominence of their dance floors, also meant that there would be an ever-present market to serve social, labor, business, and church groups both for weekend picnics and moonlight cruises. Indeed, the first boat to reach the park in 1898 was overflowing with a charter group of Detroit newsboys. Over the ensuing decades, the group market became the backbone of the Bob-lo operation.

While those newsboys enjoyed a variety of field games, a bicycle track, and a beach, the first flowering of the amusement park came with the construction of the stone building to house its first ride—the carousel, accompanied by a powerhouse to light it up and make it run. A few years later, the new dance hall, reputed to be the largest in North America, made it possible for revelers in a dance-crazy era to dance all the way to the island, all the time on the island, and all the way home. The arrival of thrill rides like the Whip, the Bug, and dodgems followed by the roller rink signaled that Bob-lo was a serious player in the developing amusement park industry.

The island's location and the economics of transportation would also critically challenge Bob-lo management through its final sixty years (1930–93). Many successes and failures of the park as a business enterprise were attributable to the abilities of the owners to adapt to the changing needs of the business of commerce, government regulations, and the recreational desires of patrons from both sides of the border. As 1930 approached, families long accustomed to taking excursion boats to recreation spots up and down the river discovered that new roads and destinations were opening up for their newly purchased automobiles. At the same time, business leaders recognized the potential for year-round cross-border commerce resulting in the opening of the Ambassador Bridge and Windsor Tunnel, directly competing for cross-river traffic with Bob-lo's owners, the Detroit and Windsor Ferry

Company. This, coupled with the Great Depression, brought the Ferry Company and Bob-lo Island to its knees.

From the day that the Ferry Company relinquished its possession of the island in the late 1930s, the Bob-lo operation was hamstrung by the very vessels that were its major source of transporting patrons to the park as well as its most visible marketing tool to the residents of its major market. Over the decades that the park was transformed from a picnic ground to a full-fledged amusement park, the one constant confronting management was the hard reality that it was located on a Canadian island and primarily accessible only by boat from Detroit in the United States. Of the seven times the park changed hands in its ninety-five-year history, only once, in 1988, was it sold without the threat of liquidation.

While dealing with several levels of the governments of two countries was part and parcel of the Ferry Company's day-to-day operations, subsequent management teams found dealing with so many layers of bureaucracy to be a burden. The boats, always expensive to operate, were perceived as a drag to the park's bottom line and became a factor in the long-range development plans of every owner from that point on. In boom times like the war years, when the economy was healthy and Detroit was fully employed, the boats were full and the park could make ends meet. But in slow years, the cost of maintaining the steamers made it difficult for park owners to secure the capital necessary for investments in park infrastructure for future growth.

From 1938 on, virtually every owner explored ideas to supplant the large vessels with smaller boats operating from locations much closer to the island. But the ultimate goal—to do away with the beloved *Columbia* and *Ste. Claire*—was regarded as a form of corporate suicide, something that owners and managers (as well as generations of patrons) could not conceive. When the locally based Browning brothers saved the steamers and park from liquidation in 1949, they saw no viable short-term alternative to continuing operation of the ships from Detroit. However, over their thirty years of stewardship, they did significantly develop the Amherstburg dock and ferry operation and laid the groundwork for an alternative system to transport patrons to the park.

When the Brownings sold Bob-lo in the late 1970s, the new out-of-town owners misjudged the special relationship that Detroiters had to the boats and Bob-lo. Their ill-timed marketing campaign and negative comments about the boats resulted in poor attendance that ultimately put the company in receivership and nearly spelled the end of the park. Just as the Browning brothers had saved the park from an untimely demise in 1949, so the Automobile Club of Michigan was able to rescue and breathe new life into the park in the 1980s. With its long-term ties to the community and deep resources, AAA management presided over Bob-lo's last flowering and was able to use its marketing savvy to positively nudge the public toward acceptance of alternate transportation to the park. The AAA plan called for fleets from both Amherstburg and Gibraltar actually capable of transporting more passengers to the island than could the venerable steamships. But when AAA sold the park in 1988 before fully implementing the plan, its new owners proved incapable of taking the necessary next steps to properly market and carry out the strategy. In retrospect, one wonders had AAA maintained control of the park and carried its strategy through, whether Bob-lo might still be operating successfully as an amusement park today.

In essence, those new owners hoped that Detroiters would simply figure out that it made better sense to drive to Amherstburg or Gibraltar. Their failure to take into account that Detroiters would need continued encouragement to go to the park from those docks can only be attributed to management's inability to do the homework necessary to understand and relate to their market. When Detroiters did not take the hint and drive to Amherstburg or Gibraltar, the owners—facing bankruptcy—chose to divest the large ships and the Detroit docks in 1991. Their fate was a well-deserved corporate suicide. Unfortunately, their behavior placed Bob-lo in mortal danger as well. With the negative publicity attendant the disposition of the *Columbia* and *Ste. Claire* in late 1991, many Detroiters assumed that the island itself had closed. Many others silently mourned the loss of the big ships by simply staying home the next season, thus sealing the fate of that company and placing the island on the auction block.

In 1993 the park's last owner—unencumbered by the burden of the Detroit boats—was able to demonstrate by shrewd marketing that it was possible to convince people to come to the island in sufficient numbers by way of Amherstburg, where he planned to concentrate all future ferry operations. However, before he could fully implement that plan and create a new life for Bob-lo, fate stepped in and ended Bob-lo island as an amusement destination forever.

A quiet summer . . . The Bob-lo sellout . . . The Wonderful World of Disney meets Bois Blanc . . . Mansions along the shore . . . The return of the First Nation . . . Bad water, bad blood . . . The end of Oram's dream . . . A vision restored?

I believe that everyone in life hungers to establish a legacy.
JOHN ORAM, BOIS BLANC ISLAND RESORT COMMUNITY BROCHURE, 1997

Summer. The 1994 season beckoned, but the island was stripped of its rides and its buildings were empty of visitors and dark for the first time since 1934. A glimmer of light was cast in August, when the Detroit Free Press proclaimed, "New Owner Wants Bob-lo Visitors Back." John Oram and his three brothers purchased Bob-lo Island, including ninety-two acres of Amherstburg dock and land properties from Northern Capital, for $2.5 million. Oram, the majority investor, came to the United States in the 1960s and built a chain of audio stores in the Detroit area. He said he wanted to turn the island into a resort-style complex with live entertainment, housing, an expanded marina, and possibly passenger boats taking people from Detroit and other spots to the island. When asked whether the handful of residents already living on the island agreed with his plan, Oram responded, "Well there's Dorothy Tresness at the back of the room," indicating the seventy-three year old who had feuded with Michael Moodenbaugh when he cut off her water from the island's filtration plant. "I've already taken Mrs. Tresness on a picnic; we went clear to the other side of the island. She said she hadn't seen it in years."[1]

Oram began putting his concept to work. He consulted with a Disney team and developed a "vision plan" for what would be called the Bois Blanc Island Resort Community. It included a canal running from the east to west side of the island to segregate the houses from a village center in the middle of the island. It also showed a significantly expanded marina as well as a golf course located where the 1926 course once stood.[2] One ride that was not sold, the 375-foot Sky Tower, remained in place. Oram maintained the dance hall, roller rink, powerhouse, and several smaller buildings, which were the only other reminders of the amusement park. The remains of the lighthouse and blockhouse continued to stand sentinel over the southern part of the island, and the Sailors Monument was still visible from the Amherstburg shore. Oram dug up an area of the White Sands to discourage rowdy partiers from encroaching on his dreamscape and scaring wealthy investors away.

Oram began subdividing and selling real estate on the northern portion of the island. In 1996 he offered fifty-two lots with prices ranging from $125,000 to $600,000. His company also controlled all construction allowed on the property. Oram's goal was to build sixty

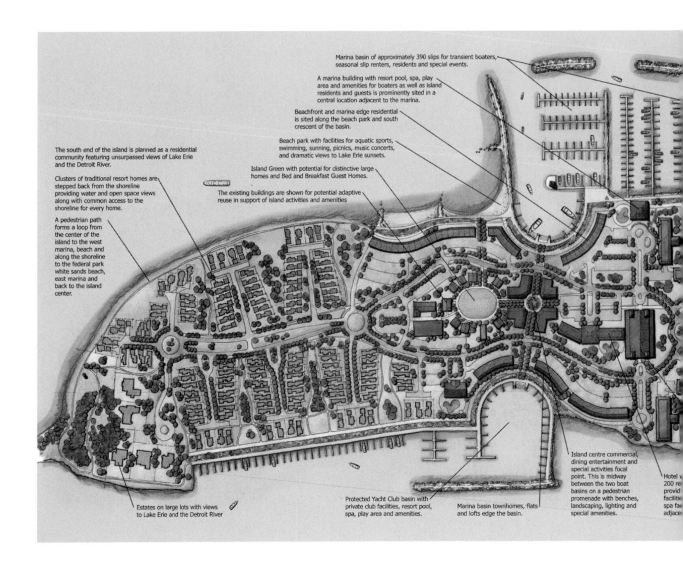

Marina basin of approximately 390 slips for transient boaters, seasonal slip renters, residents and special events.

A marina building with resort pool, spa, play area and amenities for boaters as well as island residents and guests is prominently sited in a central location adjacent to the marina.

Beachfront and marina edge residential is sited along the beach park and south crescent of the basin.

Beach park with facilities for aquatic sports, swimming, sunning, picnics, music concerts, and dramatic views to Lake Erie sunsets.

Island Green with potential for distinctive large homes and Bed and Breakfast Guest Homes.

The existing buildings are shown for potential adaptive reuse in support of island activities and amenities

The south end of the island is planned as a residential community featuring unsurpassed views of Lake Erie and the Detroit River.

Clusters of traditional resort homes are stepped back from the shoreline providing water and open space views along with common access to the shoreline for every home.

A pedestrian path forms a loop from the center of the island to the west marina, beach and along the shoreline to the federal park white sands beach, east marina and back to the island center.

Estates on large lots with views to Lake Erie and the Detroit River

Protected Yacht Club basin with private club facilities, resort pool, spa, play area and amenities.

Marina basin townhomes, flats and lofts edge the basin.

Island centre commercial, dining entertainment and special activities focal point. This is midway between the two boat basins on a pedestrian promenade with benches, landscaping, lighting and special amenities.

Hotel w 200 re provid facilitie spa fac adjace

units a year until he had a total of seven hundred. His Village Center idea evolved to a Mackinac Island–style setting with restaurants, fudge shops, horse rides, and a petting zoo and would be designed to attract daytrippers to the island's 140-slip marina.

While the layout plan showed new islets dotting the shoreline, it also featured two parcels of note. The first, identified only by a blank space, was the property once owned by James Randall for his Look-out Cottage on the north end and now owned by the Pandolfo family, who had recently constructed a large home there. The second parcel,

John Oram's 1997 Bois Blanc community plan, as enhanced by Amico Properties in 2006. In author's collection.

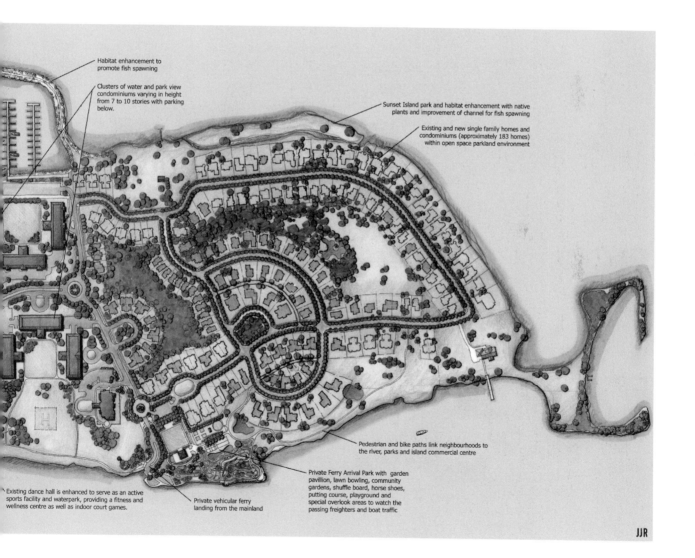

Habitat enhancement to promote fish spawning

Clusters of water and park view condominiums varying in height from 7 to 10 stories with parking below.

Sunset Island park and habitat enhancement with native plants and improvement of channel for fish spawning

Existing and new single family homes and condominiums (approximately 183 homes) within open space parkland environment

Pedestrian and bike paths link neighbourhoods to the river, parks and island commercial centre

Existing dance hall is enhanced to serve as an active sports facility and waterpark, providing a fitness and wellness centre as well as indoor court games.

Private vehicular ferry landing from the mainland

Private Ferry Arrival Park with garden pavillion, lawn bowling, community gardens, shuffle board, horse shoes, putting course, playground and special overlook areas to watch the passing freighters and boat traffic

JJR

owned and occupied by Dorothy Tresness on the west side, was included with the other lots as available for purchase. Oram, having bought and demolished an old cottage next door to hers, felt she would not hold out and had optimistically included her property in the brochure. The Tresness property was the last of the lots originally deeded from John Atkinson to J. H. Keena in 1889. By April 1997 over half of the new lots were reported as sold.[3]

The properties continued to sell well, and Bob-lo became noted for the minimansions that clustered along the shores on its northern half. Association fees included water and sewage service. Residents also paid annual fees to moor their boats at the marina and $2,500 per residence to maintain year-round ferry service from Amherstburg. Oram replaced the sewage lagoon with a new large capacity all-season sewage treatment plant the following year with the agreement that the town of Amherstburg would assume management within seven years.

In 1999 Oram announced plans for development of the town of Amherstburg. First, he envisioned a new maritime district centered around the historic King's Navy Yard. His proposal for the "Bob-lo Boardwalk" included a luxury hotel, restaurants, a 107-slip marina, and a pier for cruise ships, all set in an Epcot-style world market environment. His second plan involved the ninety-two-acre parcel of Amherstburg land used for the dock and parking that he acquired with the purchase of Bob-lo. Oram announced a long-range plan to recreate a Bob-lo Island amusement park on the site, complete with roller coasters, water rides, carnival games, and other attractions. He also spoke of plans to operate commuter boats between Detroit, Windsor, Amherstburg, Toledo, and Cleveland. Finally, he announced that he would like to permanently place the SS *Ste. Claire* at the Bob-lo Island dock.[4]

As John Oram continued to build his empire, cracks began to appear in the foundation. The first came from an almost forgotten source—the original users of the island itself. Hearkening back to the time when the British first acquired the island from the Ottawas and Chippewas in 1786, the Walpole Island First Nation issued a news release dated May 11, 2000: "Commission Finds Surrender of Aboriginal Title to Bob-lo Island Invalid." The Indian Claims Commission (ICC), an independent body established by the Canadian government in 1991 and charged with investigating disputed First Nations land claims, stated, "Our inquiry found that whatever aboriginal title to Bob-lo Island existed in 1786, still exists today." In 1786, the Crown entered into a treaty for the surrender of Bob-lo with representatives of the Ottawas and Chippewas. The First Nations historical records of that time, however, indicate the agreement was only to put the island into the Crown's hands for temporary protection from settler encroachment. The First Nations' intent was to create a reserve, not to give the lands away. Further, the ICC noted that the Crown failed to involve other tribes that had legitimate claim to the island and that the surrender did not take place in a public meeting as dictated by Royal Proclamation. The ICC also discovered that a subsequent treaty in 1790, designed to address the questionable nature of several similar government land surrenders, failed to include Bob-lo Island. The 1786 surrender of Bob-lo was deemed illegal and invalid, and the ICC recommended that the First Nations submit a claim through the courts to clarify title to the island.

Because Canadian government policy does not include displacement of third parties in title disputes, there was no direct threat to Oram or the residents of Bob-lo. Nevertheless, the negative publicity contributed to slowed sales of properties on the island. Oram never broke ground on his Bob-lo Boardwalk in Amherstburg, and the ideas for the amusement park and the *Ste. Claire* quietly vanished.[5]

Unfortunately for Oram, with daylong waits at the bridge and tunnel leading local news, U.S. citizens began thinking twice about investing in vacation homes in Canada. Shortly after September 11, 2001, the newly formed U.S. Department of Homeland Security mandated that U.S. boaters traveling to Canadian ports needed to possess entry documents for every passenger for every trip. The requirement made it not quite worth the trip to Bob-lo for most day travelers from the United States, and, as a result, business at the island marina dried up, and the restaurant closed soon after. That also spelled trouble for Oram's vision of the daytrippers who would someday flock to the island's yet unbuilt Village Center.

But Oram showed his resiliency in 2002 when he initiated construction of a five-story, thirty-nine-unit condo development located near the Sailors Monument. The Amherstburg Town Council, however, refused Oram's proposal to build a new water park on the parking lot and dock property in Amherstburg.[6] A few months later, in a scene reminiscent of the Atkinson-Randall dispute of 1894, Oram initiated a lawsuit to block the Pandolfo family's attempts to subdivide their own property and build new residences on the north end of the island.

Then another problem surfaced: the Ontario Ministry of Environment charged that Bob-lo's owners and a private testing lab had failed to report potentially deadly bacteria in their aging water plant in September 2000. The bacteria were the same that had killed seven and sickened hundreds that same year in Walkerton, Ontario. The government immediately turned operation of the plant over to the Ontario Clean Water Act and began an investigation to determine why Oram and the testing lab had failed to report the problem.[7] The Amherstburg Town Council, concerned for the safety of Bob-lo residents and taxpayers, began debating the installation of a water pipeline under the river. At the core of the debate was whether Oram and company should shoulder a portion of the costs for the line.

That December, John Pandolfo won the right to proceed with his development plans as well as the right to access the island sewage and water systems. Oram argued that they had an agreement and that this would obstruct the water views of several of his properties and lower their value. Pandolfo responded that there never was any such agreement and proceeded to put his lots on the market.[8]

As 2003 rolled around, the quarrel was rekindled when Oram refused to allow the Pandolfos or their guests to ride the ferry to or from the mainland. As a result, Pandolfo's buyers backed out of their agreements to buy his property. It was only because of provincial law that Oram was forced to allow the Pandolfo children to ride the ferry to and from school. The argument soon immersed much of Amherstburg in a discussion that revolved around the use of tax dollars in support of what was perceived as the private island community. When some town council members argued that the people on Bob-lo were paying good tax dollars and deserved services, others rejoined that the parkland of Bob-lo should be as open as were the streets and parks of Amherstburg. While the town officials refused to mediate the ferry access dispute, the issue was kept alive indirectly through the debate over who should pay for the proposed waterline. Although an anticipated government grant would cover about two-thirds of the $1.5 million cost of the waterline, the argument centered on how quickly Oram should be expected to repay the town for the balance.[9]

The debate continued for the duration of the year until it was overshadowed by Oram's Christmas announcement for a partnership to develop up to one thousand new houses on Bob-lo. His strategy was to merge with a large real estate concern while remaining president and CEO of his organization. The plan still contained the essential components of his vision, including the Village Center, the difference being that a lot more houses would be built around it. He expressed a desire to work closely with the town of Amherstburg to the benefit of all parties.[10]

The waterline issue seesawed back and forth over the winter of 2004 but was kicked off the front page by a May announcement that the companies of Bob-lo were in receivership. John Oram's brother Randy, a minority partner, had launched the court action that led to this juncture. John Oram claimed surprise and disappointment at this development just as they were in the final stages of completing a restructuring deal that would put their Bob-lo Island holdings in a secure position for long-term growth and stability. He stated that he would remain active in management, that the company would stay open for business, that the ferry would continue to run, and that the island would continue to be maintained at a high standard. Oram blamed the slowdown in sales and cash flow to the border crossing difficulties precipitated by the aftermath of September 11, 2001. He stated that those problems had finally been resolved and that he was looking forward to their future plans for Bob-lo.[11]

The announcement gave proof to the rumors that had been swirling around the island community and Amherstburg for some time. There was much talk in the community that Oram had been having difficulty paying builders and contractors since the sales slowdown began, and many contractors were refusing to work with him until paid for past work. The five-story condo near the dock had now been standing unfinished two years after construction started. By this time, many residents expressed concern over the possible completion of the golf course and village center, fearing that their assessments would skyrocket. This was not quite the paradise they had been promised.

In early August the Amherstburg Town Council awarded the contract to install the waterline to Bob-lo to Amico Contracting and Engineering. At the same time, the Ontario Clean Water Act, overseers of the Amherstburg-operated Bob-lo water plant, reported leakage of raw water due to decay in the facility and placed a boil water advisory on Bob-lo residences. The Amherstburg Town Council, acutely aware of the situation, voted to recover the costs of the pipeline from the Oram companies within forty-five days of installation.[12]

Less than a week later the report of the court-appointed receiver was released and detailed claims filed by Randy Oram against John Oram, Gary Oram, and eight limited partnerships that constituted the Bob-lo holding companies. The report described all claims and approved amounts as well as a prioritized procedure for claimants to cast votes to elect a new owner for Bob-lo. Based on the claims review, the company with the most secured claims (over 50 percent) was Amico Contracting and Engineering. The report also identified that property sales declined after the 2000 fiscal year and that they lost $1.5 million in 2001 and $3.1 million in 2003. The company was relying largely on shareholders to support cash flow needs.[13]

On a brighter note, Dorothy Tresness, who rebuffed Oram's offer to buy her out years earlier, now resurfaced with a successful suit to access the island's water. Once indoor plumbing was installed the eighty-four year old would at last have an alternative to bathing in the river. And, since her suit awarded her rights to all utilities, she would also enjoy electricity for the first time without having to run an electric cord to her neighbor's house. She could do nothing, however, about the barrier of trees that Oram had planted around the outside perimeter of her cottage.

As the summer of 2004 drew to a close, the ferry service reverted to a pay as you go venture, and most residents, fearing being stranded on the island, chose to stay in their shoreside homes. The island full of houses was eerily empty through the warmest days of the year, a time when only a decade before it was at its fullest. As it had been so many times over the past century, the fate of the new owner of Bob-lo Island would be settled by the courts.

In late November 2004, ownership of the island was awarded to Dominic Amicone, the construction company owner who was first among Oram's creditors. Through the process of receivership, he wasted little time in making the island again accessible to the long-frustrated property owners. By early 2006 he had rebuilt the ferry service, reopened the marina restaurant to the public, and began completing and selling the five-story condos. His plan, refashioning Oram's, was to develop up to fifteen hundred residences, townhouses, and condos over the next several years and to build a small village in the center of the island anchored by the amusement building and powerhouse, with restaurants and shops open to the public. A Leamington native, Amicone's vision was to provide a place for the public to dance and recreate on Bob-lo once again. His success as an engineer and developer throughout Ontario gave the people of Amherstburg hope that the island would once again come alive.[14]

The END of a PERFECT DAY

THE SUN is setting as the last boat leaves Bob-Lo. Up the cool, mysterious river drives the steamer. Blast furnaces gleam red against the darkening sky. The moon is up and those who are not dancing enjoy the evening breeze on the outside decks. The sky-line of Detroit looks weird in the moonlight. The Border Cities flash thousands of lamps. The boat edges toward the wharf and is made fast. The pleasure-filled crowd tumbles out, to wend their respective ways home. A red-letter day has passed. A day which has made thousands of people supremely happy.

BOB-LO THE GREATEST SPOT ON EARTH

And thus Bob-lo Island sits today: a partially developed landscape with Victorian houses slowly replacing the succession of trees that sheltered midnight dances, coureurs de bois, British sentries, grazing sheep, lazy Sunday picnics, and a century's worth of summer dreams. While Detroit newspapers provide updates on the status of the efforts to save the *Columbia* and the *Ste. Claire,* reports from the island lament the collapsed state of the last of the 1838 blockhouses.[1]

Over time Bob-lo Island has been a place of opportunity and respite for the peoples of the region. The First Nation tribes found it a convenient place to restore their energies and plan for the common good. The French explorers knew it as source of excellent wood, and their missionaries as a place to harvest souls. The British saw it as a place to control both commerce and the approach of adversaries. The first private owners developed Bob-lo as a place devoted to rest and relaxation. Over the course of the twentieth century, many business-people sought to make a living by maintaining the park as an island of refuge and entertainment for the masses of the growing metropolis upriver.

And it is these masses who came generation after generation to regard the island as theirs. These families responded by the millions to the whistle's blasts to ride the large white boats down the river to "The Greatest Spot on Earth." Once there, they carried their picnic baskets to a shelter, and the kids began their exploration of the island. First, to see what was old—the lighthouse, the blockhouse, the anchor—and, for the more adventuresome, to search for traces of the grandstands or even the cafeteria or old mansions. Then the searchers turned to the midway to test the newest rides and attractions. Perhaps most significant to the children engaged in these explorations was that, except for the very youngest, there was minimal parental supervision or involvement. Because it was "owned" by the patrons, the entire island of Bob-lo was considered a safe place for young people to explore and learn about the larger world. The scary streets of Detroit were both out of sight and out of mind. Especially in its later years, Bob-lo was one of the few venues in the metropolitan area where people of every color could be found recreating together in a shared environment. For all of its flaws, Bob-lo was a model of diversity before the word became fashionable.

In retrospect, there is good reason for Detroiters to recall Bob-lo with fond memories to this day. Those memories were abetted by the thousands of people from both sides of the border who dedicated the better parts of their lives to the management and maintenance of the island. Those people of Detroit and Amherstburg who were the park managers, engineers, ride operators, ships' crews, concession workers, and maintenance staff were there before, during, and after the park was open to the public. And especially to the people of Amherstburg Bob-lo has meaning as a place of both opportunity and respite. They were provided a firsthand view of how the island could positively affect the lives of everyone who set foot there, employee and patron alike.

Maynard Hurst, an Amherstburg minister and former park employee, says he has heard that the last park owner, Michael Moodenbaugh, is recovering from his 1993 accident and is doing better now. He expresses a hope that Moodenbaugh would somehow be able to return and fulfill his promise to make the park come to life once again. More than a dozen years after the last amusement park proponent left the scene, Hurst is not alone among people in Amherstburg who still hold out hope for another Bob-lo summertime hero. Of course, eight hundred summer jobs meant a lot to a small town like Amherstburg that has seen its industrial base erode severely over the past decades. Hurst, a one-time member of the island winter work gang, observed, "A lot of Amherstburg kids benefited from work on Bob-lo. Young people need opportunities. That is what hurts my heart because what we want is simply opportunities for our kids."[2] Another former park customer relations manager and Amherstburg resident, Ted Diesbourg, was optimistic about the survival of the Bob-lo spirit: "I still have hopes that we can open another park in this area. Bob-lo provided summer jobs for hundreds of kids in this area as well as a place for families to go. The community needs something and the kids need something too."[3]

Thanks in large part to the combined efforts of the people of Detroit and Amherstburg, Bob-lo Island survived as a Detroit area amusement park long after other area parks had been forced to shut down. Although none of the local owners or park employees became wealthy in the process, most managed to make a living. Along the way, the park also served to acculturate almost a million patrons annually while providing jobs and college funding for thousands of people in the region. It is both amazing and sad that, in this region of six million people

(Opposite page)
Bob-lo Island in 2006.
Photograph courtesy Bois Blanc Marina
Resort Community.

seeking local, affordable family destinations, nothing has emerged to fill the void left by the park's closure. Those people who succeeded in keeping the vision of Bob-lo Island alive as an amusement park over the decades should be regarded as everyday heroes for the moments of fun, adventure, and pleasure they provided for generations of families.

Although the memories of Bob-lo will fade, there is an opportunity in this area for someone to help create a living monument to the spirit of Bob-lo. A place where people from two countries can once again gather to celebrate the joys of summer in sight of the beautiful river that connects us.

NOTES

Chapter 1

1. A wide variety of trees are attributed to the white wood, or *bois blanc,* that gave the island its name. Many instinctively attribute the wood in question to birch or aspen. Yet, in the 1700s the area forest was predominantly Carolinian and would not have featured either of those species in any abundance. Bill Casselman, in *Casselman's Canadian Words: A Comic Browse through Words and Folk Sayings Invented by Canadians* (Toronto: McArthur, 1997), cites the basswood (or linden) as the tree commonly referred to as "bois blanc" by the coureurs de bois, the French trappers who made their living in the woods and wetlands of the frontier. While basswood itself is not whitish in exterior appearance, its interior lumber was noted for its whiteness by the coureurs, who were dependent upon wood more for its utility than its appearance. *Michigan Trees,* by Burton Barnes and Warren Wagner (Ann Arbor: University of Michigan Press, 1981; p. 108), and *The Michigan Pioneer and Historical Collection* (Washington, DC: Library of Congress, 1887; vol. 12, p. 380) both corroborate the use of the term "bois blanc" to describe the basswood tree. This calls into question the popular assertion that the French name of the island derives from a Huron Indian phrase that was translated by the Jesuit Pierre Potier in his 1751 *Elementary Huron Grammar,* almost a century after the coureurs de bois began passing through and describing the area. Potier asserted that the Huron name for the island was Etiowiteendannenti, which his dictionary translated as "a peopled island of white woods guarding the entrance." As this was coincident with the first recorded habitation of the island (by the Jesuit mission), Potier may have attempted to translate a French description for the island into the Huron rather than the opposite. Kay Givens-McGowan, in her essay "The Wyandot and the River" (in *Honoring Our Detroit River: Caring for Our Home,* ed. John H. Hartig, 23–34 [Bloomfield Hills, MI: Cranbrook Institute of Science, 2003]), states that the Wyandots (also known as the Hurons) called the island Atieeronnon, which translated to "the place of the white ash tree people." I am more inclined to agree with this as being more in accord with how the Wyandots—themselves transplanted to the island—would have described the place for themselves.

2. Ernest J. LaJeunesse, *The Windsor Border Region, Canada's Southernmost Frontier: A Collection of Documents* (Toronto: University of Toronto Press, 1960); W. H. Smith, *Canada: Past, Present and Future* (Toronto: T. Maclear, 1851), 5. LaJeunesse cites the *Potier Gazette* (1747; Le College Ste.

Marie Archives, Montreal, Quebec), which specifically states, "There-upon the missionary settled most of the tribe on the neighboring Isle aux Bois Blanc and on the adjacent mainland on the east side of the river. This event took place on October 13, 1742." The *Gazette* also states that the mission house was located on the island and is the source for the census of the island mission in 1747.

3. References are drawn from Daniel G. Hill, *The Freedom-Seekers: Blacks in Early Canada* (Toronto: Stoddart, 1992), 13; Indian Claims Commission as reported in Walpole Island First Nation news release, "Commission Finds Surrender Invalid," May 11, 2000; David Botsford, "The History of Bois Blanc Island," *Ontario History Magazine* 47 (Summer 1955); and LaJeunesse, *Windsor Border Region*. Some of the dates given in these texts conflict, but the basic sequence of events is agreed upon by all authors.

4. Isaac Weld, Jr., *Travels through the States of North America and the Provinces of Upper and Lower Canada* (London: John Stockdale, 1840), 343.

5. Hill, *Freedom-Seekers*.

6. Bob-lo Lighthouse File, Marsh Collection Society, Amherstburg, Ontario (hereafter cited as Marsh Collection Society).

7. William Moffett, *The Story of Bob-lo* (Detroit: Bob-lo Excursion Company, 1943). Variants of this story appear in several texts about Bois Blanc found in the Marsh Collection Society. One version of the story adds that Mrs. Hackett was related to the lighthouse architect, Andrew Kemp, and may have used the connection to petition the governor on her husband's behalf. *Amherstburg, 1796–1996: The New Town on the Garrison Grounds, Book I* (Amherstburg, ON: Amherstburg Bicentennial Book Committee, 1996).

8. Smith, *Canada: Past, Present and Future*.

9. Dennis Carter-Edwards, *Fort Malden: A Structural Narrative History, 1796–1976*, vol. 1 (N.p.: Parks Canada, 1980); Newspaper clipping, *Detroit Advertiser and Tribune*, July 25, 1874, Detroit Public Library. See also Ordnance Land Contract for Rankin purchase of Bois Blanc Island, Essex County, Province of Ontario, Canada, recorded September 29, 1874, copy in Marsh Collection Society.

10. David Beasley, *Alexander McKee and the Heyday of the American Theater*, (Waterloo, ON: Laurier University Press, 2004), 1–12, 120.

11. Newspaper clipping, *Detroit Advertiser and Tribune*, July 25, 1874, Detroit Public Library; Ordnance Land Contract for Rankin purchase of Bois Blanc Island, Marsh Collection Society.

12. Newspaper clipping, *Amherstburg (ON) Echo*, April 9, 1875, scrapbook, Marsh Collection Society.

13. Gordon Bugbee, "Stars on the River," *Steamboat Bill Magazine* (Winter 2001): 256–93, quote at 264.

14. Ibid., 283. Also see Gordon Bugbee, *The Coming of the Tashmoo*, a pamphlet prepared for the Columbia Labor Day cruise of 1976. Dossin Great Lakes Museum of the Detroit Historical Museum, Belle Isle, Michigan (hereafter cited as Dossin Museum).

15. Botsford, "History of Bois Blanc Island."

16. Newspaper clipping, Bob-lo File (River Section), Burton Historical Collection, Detroit Public Library, Detroit, Michigan.

17. Deed of Land, County of Essex, Province of Ontario, recorded May 29, 1888, copy in Marsh Collection Society; Newspaper clipping, *Amherstburg (ON) Echo,* July 1, 1887, scrapbook, Marsh Collection Society.

18. Newspaper clippings, *Amherstburg (ON) Echo,* November 25, 1887, and June 1, 1888, scrapbook, Marsh Collection Society.

19. Fitzgerald was pleased to be able to use the island for important meetings of his executive committee, where "importunate reporters would not intercede upon their deliberations." *Detroit Evening News,* October 22, 1891, Randall paper, Burton Historical Collection.

20. James Randall Papers, vols. 43 and 63, Burton Historical Collection, Detroit Public Library, Detroit, Michigan (hereafter cited as Randall Papers).

21. *Detroit Evening News,* October 15, 1891, Randall papers, Burton Historical Collection.

22. Newspaper clipping, *Amherstburg (ON) Echo,* September 14, 1894, scrapbook, Marsh Collection Society.

23. "War on Bois Blanc," *Detroit Free Press,* January 25, 1895; Randall Papers. See also Newspaper clipping, *Amherstburg (ON) Echo,* January 25, 1895, scrapbook, Marsh Collection Society.

24. Newspaper clipping, *Amherstburg (ON) Echo,* March 30, 1900, scrapbook, Marsh Collection Society. In the midst of this turmoil, Randall's young son Tom was lost to the river while duck hunting near Lookout Cottage. Tom's body was eventually recovered near Sugar Island. The Randall family conducted many subsequent conversations with the boy through a medium in the living room of the cottage, where his image was engraved on the glass of the front door. Randall Papers.

Chapter 2

1. *Detroit News,* December 25, 1894, Detroit, Belle Isle, and Windsor Ferry Company Scrapbook, Dossin Museum (hereafter cited as Ferry Company Scrapbook). Also see Jack Schramm and William Henning, *Detroit's Street Railways: Volume 1, 1863–1922* (Chicago: Central Electric Railfans Association, 1978), 35–50. Detroit's private streetcar companies were consolidated into Detroit United Railways in 1900.

2. William Oxford, *The Ferry Steamers* (Toronto: Boston Mills, 2002), 118–21. The appendices provide several colorful examples of Campbell's character and management style.

3. Ferry Company Scrapbook, 1896. Also see Michael M. Dixon, *When Detroit Rode the Waves: A Summer Cruise along the Detroit and St. Clair Rivers Aboard the Riverboats of the Early 20th Century* (Grosse Pointe Farms, MI: Mervue Publications, 2001), 18–20.

4. Bugbee, "Stars on the River," 275–77.

5. Ibid.

6. Newspaper clippings, Ferry Company Scrapbook, 1897–98; *Detroit Free Press*, December 19, 1997.

7. *Windsor (ON) Evening Record*, April 11, 1898, and May 7, 1898.

8. "Beautiful Bois Blanc," *Detroit News-Tribune*, June 5, 1898.

9. Almost missed in the hoopla was an ad in a German-language paper in which the name "Boys Blank" (a mishearing of Bois Blanc) stood out as the only non-German words. Ferry Company Scrapbook, 1898.

10. I have used Bugbee, *Coming of the Tashmoo*, for information regarding the *Tashmoo*. I have also used the Ferry Company Scrapbook for newspaper accounts regarding the competition to their enterprise.

11. I have used Oxford, *Ferry Steamers*, for reference regarding the Detroit, Belle Isle, and Windsor ferries.

12. "St. Andrews Picnic: Trouble on the Docks," *Amherstburg (ON) Echo*, August 17, 1901.

13. Ferry Company Scrapbook, July 1902; Newspaper clipping, *Amherstburg (ON) Echo*, July 7, 1902, scrapbook, Marsh Collection Society.

14. "Red Hot Race Down the River: *Columbia* Beats the *Kirby*," *Detroit Free Press*, August 1902.

Chapter 3

1. Gordon Bugbee, "Ballroom Boats," *Telescope Magazine* (May 2000).

2. Oxford, *Ferry Steamers*, 110.

3. Newspaper clipping, *Detroit Free Press*, December 1897, Ferry Company Scrapbook.

4. "Stopped New Dance: Ping Pong Tabooed by Ferry Company," *Detroit News*, June 24, 1902.

5. Newspaper clippings, *Amherstburg (ON) Echo*, September 1905 and March 1906, scrapbook, Marsh Collection Society; Ferry Company Scrapbook, February 27, 1906. The Amusement Building originally housed the carousel. It became the roller rink in the 1940s and was converted to a theater for magic shows in the 1980s.

6. Newspaper ad clipping, August 1906, Ferry Company Scrapbook.

7. The case had its lighter moments, such as when the ship's purser, Charles Park, volunteered to demonstrate the rag dance in court for an inquisitive judge. Newspaper clippings, *Detroit News*, August 31, 1906, and September 5, 1906, Ferry Company Scrapbook.

8. Newspaper clipping, *Detroit News*, August 31, 1907, Ferry Company Scrapbook. Campbell's dedication to the more civilized masses did not go unrecognized. The Women's Cottage on Bois Blanc was described in 1907 as "an ideal place for the little ones to get fresh air and tempered sunshine. Here also are slumber rooms for those who need their daily naps. A very obliging motherly matron is also in attendance. This Women's Cottage alone is enough to give Bois Blanc a unique name on being

a family park." Newspaper clipping, *Detroit News Tribune,* July 7, 1907, Ferry Company Scrapbook.

9. Newspaper clipping, *Amherstburg (ON) Echo,* January 17, 1908, scrapbook, Marsh Collection Society; Michigan Supreme Court proceedings, November 2, 1908 (transcript in Detroit, Belle Isle, and Windsor Ferry Company Minutes Index, Dossin Museum [hereafter cited as Ferry Company Minutes]).

10. Newspaper clipping, *Amherstburg (ON) Echo,* July 17, 1908, scrapbook, Marsh Collection Society.

11. Newspaper clipping, *Amherstburg (ON) Echo,* September 18, 1908, scrapbook, Marsh Collection Society.

12. "Why Not White Wood?" *Detroit Journal,* as reprinted in the *Amherstburg (ON) Echo,* February 4, 1909, scrapbook, Marsh Collection Society. See also chapter 1, note 1.

13. Newspaper clippings, *Amherstburg (ON) Echo,* October 22 and December 10, 1909, scrapbook, Marsh Collection Society.

14. Ferry Company Minutes, January 1912.

15. Ibid., August 18 and 21, 1911, January 3 and 17, 1912. Kahn and Scott maintained two separate practices and offices in Detroit, and there is no indication from the Ferry Company that Kahn played any role in the design of the building.

16. Newspaper clippings, *Amherstburg (ON) Echo,* February 6, 1912, and September 27, 1912, scrapbook, Marsh Collection Society; Ferry Company Minutes, January 1913.

17. Newspaper clipping, *Amherstburg (ON) Echo,* October 25, 1912, scrapbook, Marsh Collection Society.

18. Newspaper clippings, *Amherstburg (ON) Echo,* July 5 and 23, 1912, and May 23, 1913, scrapbook, Marsh Collection Society. While reports of the planned resort for the Randall property appeared as early as 1908 (see, e.g., "Bois Blanc to Have Swell Club House," *Windsor (ON) Evening Record,* November 2, 1908), physical evidence of Point Bob-lo itself remains something of a mystery. There is no indication that the proposed structures were ever built, and the Randall cottage stood on the site until it burned in 1931. It is the author's conjecture that the so-called Menzies Hotel was actually converted from the Randall cottage.

19. "New Mammoth Dancing Pavilion on Bob-lo Island," *Windsor (ON) Evening Record,* June 7, 1913.

20. Ferry Company Minutes, January 1914.

Chapter 4

1. Newspaper clipping, *Amherstburg (ON) Echo,* August 26, 1913, scrapbook, Marsh Collection Society; "Ferry Co. Plans for Peche Isle," *Windsor (ON) Evening Record,* August 26, 1913.

2. Detroit and Windsor Ferry Company Annual Report, January 1916, Dossin Museum (hereafter cited as Ferry Company Annual Report). The gov-

ernment inspection came only months after the greatest ship-related tragedy in the history of the Great Lakes, when the excursion vessel *Eastland*
capsized at dock in the Chicago River, sending more than fifteen hundred
passengers to their deaths. The Eastland had a reputation among sailors
as a "wobbler," and fate finally caught up with her on a sunny summer
morning. Since that time, the U.S. Inspection Service had been much
more rigid in their examination of passenger ships.

3. Ibid., January 1918.

4. Ibid., January 1920.

5. Ferry Company Annual Report, January 1920.

6. Ibid., January 1921. See also Hartig, *Honoring Our Detroit River*, 62–65.

7. Ferry Company Annual Report, January 1922.

8. Ibid., January 1923.

9. Obituary of Walter Campbell, *Border Cities Star* (Windsor, ON), September 10, 1923.

10. As reprinted in Oxford, *Ferry Steamers*, 83.

11. Ferry Company Annual Report, January 1924.

12. Ibid., January 1926.

13. Bugbee, "Stars on the River," 289.

14. "Burg Ferry to Quit Run," *Border Cities Star* (Windsor, ON), May 28,
1925.

15. "Storm of Protest Expected from Amherstburg as Result," *Border Cities
Star* (Windsor, ON), May 28, 1925.

16. Newspaper clipping, *Amherstburg (ON) Echo*, May 24, 1925, scrapbook,
Marsh Collection Society.

17. Ferry Company Minutes, 1927. See also Newspaper clipping, *Amherstburg (ON) Echo*, October 25, 1995, scrapbook, Marsh Collection Society.

18. "Stone Building Built to House Little Auto Coasters," *Amherstburg (ON)
Echo*, March 30, 1928. The new dodgems building would be 100 x 28
feet.

19. Detroit and Windsor Ferry Company Ledger, 1924–32, Dossin Museum
(hereafter cited as Ferry Company Ledger).

20. *Billboard Magazine*, February 1, 1930.

21. "Old Randall Mansion on Bois Blanc Island Totally Destroyed in Daylight
Fire," *Amherstburg (ON) Echo*, September 4, 1931. The article stated, "Old
residents of Amherstburg still remember the picture of Thomas Randall
which was engraved on the stained glass in the front door of the Randall mansion and was said to have been impressed there by supernatural
agencies." See also Newspaper clipping, *Detroit News*, September 1, 1931,
Ferry Company Scrapbook.

22. Philip Mason, *Rumrunning and the Roaring Twenties: Prohibition on the
Michigan-Ontario Waterway* (Detroit: Wayne State University Press, 1995),
154.

23. Ferry Company Ledger, 1932.

24. Newspaper clipping, *Amherstburg (ON) Echo*, March 30, 1933, scrapbook,
Marsh Collection Society; Newspaper clipping, *Detroit News*, April 5,
1933, Ferry Company Scrapbook.

25. Ferry Company Annual Report, January 1934.

26. Newspaper clipping, *Detroit News,* April 5, 1933, Ferry Company Scrapbook.

27. "New Pleasure Resort North End of Bob-lo," *Amherstburg (ON) Echo,* September 14, 1934.

28. Ibid. Island Lines board members included John R. Kerby of Grosse Pointe Farms and John Atkinson of Detroit. The area created by the fill became known as Duncanson Bay.

29. "Happy New Year for Everyone," *Amherstburg (ON) Echo,* January 1935.

30. Ferry Company Annual Report, January 1935. It could be surmised that Mr. Paddock was speaking in reference to Bob-lo's claim in the Meisner case of 1908, when a distinction was made between the public conveyance of the cross-river ferry operation and the operation of the private park on Bob-lo. In support of his concern and tucked away in the back of the Ferry Company's index to the minutes was a copy of the State of Michigan Public Act 1919, No. 375, the Michigan Equal Rights Act, which states, in part, "All persons within the jurisdiction of this State shall be entitled to full and equal accommodations, advantages, facilities and privileges of inns, restaurants, eating houses, barber shops, public conveyances on land and water."

31. Bugbee, "Stars on the River," 293.

32. Coleman Young and Lonnie Wheeler, *Hard Stuff: The Autobiography of Mayor Coleman Young* (New York: Viking Penguin, 1994), 30.

33. Ferry Company Ledger, 1935.

34. Ibid.

35. Ferry Company Annual Report, January 1937.

36. "Bob-lo Steamers Get State Beer License," *Detroit Free Press,* May 20, 1937.

37. Ferry Company Minutes, September 17, 1937.

38. Ibid.

39. Addendum to Vance memo, ibid.

40. Ibid.

Chapter 5

1. Oxford, *Ferry Steamers,* 96.

2. Ferry Company Minutes, August 12, 1938.

3. Oxford, *Ferry Steamers,* 114.

4. Bob-lo Steamers Incorporated Minutes, September 1938 (hereafter cited as Bob-lo Minutes). The Bob-lo Minutes are located with the Ferry Company Minutes at the Dossin Museum.

5. Bob-lo Minutes, January 11, 1939.

6. Chicago, Duluth, and Georgian Bay Transit Company (Georgian Bay Line) Shareholders Meeting Minutes, February 2, 1939, Miscellaneous Box 75, Burton Historical Collection, Detroit Public Library, Detroit, Michigan (hereafter cited as GBL Minutes). The proposed contract had

eight points. The second stated: "It is understood that no negro be carried and no slot machines installed and no hard liquor sold." Bob-lo Minutes, February 1939.

7. Newspaper clipping, *Detroit Free Press*, February 23, 1939, Ferry Company Scrapbook.

8. Bob-lo Minutes, May 1939.

9. "Bob-lo Steamers Start 41st Season," *Detroit Free Press*, June 11, 1939.

10. "Bob-lo Invaded, 4 Net $10,000," *Detroit Free Press*, June 11, 1939. After the gang conducted a successful repeat performance the following year, Superintendent Park elected to keep the day's receipts out of the safe and had employees hide them under their cots in the boy's dorm located on the second floor of the Log Cabin. Ted Gatfield, interview, September 2004.

11. *Billboard Magazine*, July 15, 1939.

12. "Bob-lo Does Best in a Decade," *Billboard Magazine*, September 15, 1939.

13. GBL Minutes, December 31, 1939.

14. Fletcher's family had been involved in Great Lakes lumbering and shipping for over a century. Originally located along the St. Clair River, they followed the forests and lumbering to Alpena in the 1850s. Although their company was based in Alpena, the Fletchers maintained interest in Detroit shipping as board members of the Detroit and Windsor Ferry Company. Harry married the sister of the late Ferry Company president Ralph Gilchrist and maintained residence in Grosse Pointe. During the winter the Fletchers managed Club Bob-lo, which offered bowling and a café and was located on property adjacent the Woodward docks. Steve Fletcher (grandson of Harry Fletcher), interview, August 2003.

15. Bob-lo files, Dossin Museum.

16. GBL Minutes, May 9, 1940.

17. Newspaper clipping, *Amherstburg (ON) Echo*, July 5, 1940, scrapbook, Marsh Collection Society; Ted Gatfield, interview, September 2004.

18. "Bob-lo Island Is Up 10% Despite Handicapped Start," *Billboard Magazine*, September 21, 1940.

19. Virginia Barclay, interview, July 2004.

20. GBL Minutes, September 24, 1941.

21. "Cold, Tired, and Hungry," *Windsor (ON) Daily Star*, June 10, 1941, 3.

22. *Windsor (ON) Star*, June 26, 1942; Tom Hamilton, interview, August 2003.

23. "Overemployment Causes Business Slump," *Billboard Magazine*, September 1942; "Parks Report Labor Shortage," *Billboard Magazine*, March 13, 1943. Strikes and crew pay issues continued to affect the industry throughout the decade. Chicago, Duluth, and Georgian Bay Transit Company personnel records stated that "growing unionization is creating problems and communists are infiltrating the National Maritime Union." To punctuate their concern, a strike delayed the start of the 1944 season for the *North American* and the *South American*. Chicago, Duluth, and Georgian Bay Transit Company Personnel Files, Burton Historical Col-

lection, Georgian Bay Line Personnel Box 78.15, Detroit Public Library, Detroit, Michigan.

24. Bill Marentette, interview, April 2003; Bob-lo Files, Dossin Museum.

25. Bob-lo Excursion Company Comparison Chart, 1942–1946, Bob-lo Files, Dossin Museum. To add to the mix during the war years, the *Detroit Free Press* reported that the Detroit vice squad caught bartenders serving beer to minors on Labor Day on the *Ste. Claire*. Not to be outdone, the *Put-in-Bay* was busted for running both booze and gambling on cruises. "Bob-lo Opens," *Detroit Free Press,* June 5, 1943.

26. Marilyn Robertson, interview, September 2004.

27. Alfred McClung Lee and Norman D. Humphrey, *Race Riot: Detroit, 1943* (New York: Octagon Books, 1943).

28. Mary Greenfield quoted in Irene Rosemond, ed., *Reflections: An Oral History of Detroit* (Detroit: Broadside Press, 1992), 21; Ted Gatfield, interview, September 2004; Tom Hamilton, interview, August 2003.

29. "New Sugar Island Park Announced," *Billboard Magazine,* February 24, 1945; "Detroit Negro Spot Opening," *Billboard Magazine,* March 10, 1945.

30. "Court Overrules Bob-lo Bias," *Michigan Chronicle,* April 26, 1947; "Bob-lo Firm Sued Again," *Pittsburgh Courier,* June 28, 1947; "Court Outlaws Bob-lo Bias," *Pittsburgh Courier,* February 7, 1948.

31. Ted Gatfield, interview, July 2004.

32. "Labor Grief May Shut Park," *Windsor (ON) Star,* April 19, 1947.

33. "Bob-lo Race Ban Nullified," *Detroit News,* April 18, 1947.

34. "Court Overrules Bob-lo Bias," *Michigan Chronicle,* April 26, 1947.

35. "Bob-lo Firm Wins Hearing," *Detroit News,* October 27, 1947.

36. "Bob-lo Discrimination Ruled Out: Excursion Firm Loses in High Court," *Detroit Free Press,* February 3, 1948.

37. U.S. Supreme Court, *Bob-lo Excursion Co. v. People of State of Michigan 333 U.S. (1948).*

38. "Bob-lo Discrimination Ruled Out."

39. *Grosse Ile Camera,* April 20, 1959.

40. "Those Trips to Bob-lo Are Now in 50th Year," *Detroit Free Press,* June 19, 1948.

41. "Dies in Windsor: Former Head of Bob-lo Island," *Amherstburg (ON) Echo,* August 25, 1956.

42. "Boat Smoke Smudges City," *Detroit Free Press,* July 31, 1948; Art Herrala, interview, September 2003.

43. "Bob-lo Faces End of Long Service: Stockholders Vote to Liquidate," *Detroit Free Press,* December 30, 1948; Newspaper clipping, *Amherstburg (ON) Echo,* December 21, 1948, scrapbook, Marsh Collection Society. In the February 7, 1949, GBL Minutes, Harry Fletcher, with his Bob-lo operation for sale, emerged for the first time as a stockholder for the Chicago, Duluth, and Georgian Bay Transit Company.

Chapter 6

1. "Bob-lo Line Sold to Lake Carriers Firm," *Detroit Free Press*, May 1, 1949, April 8, 1949; "Bob-lo Island Steamers Sold," *Detroit News*, May 1, 1949; Chuck Bade, interview, November 2003.

2. Bill Browning, interview, November 2003.

3. "Cruising Down To Bob-lo," *Detroit Free Press*, May 16, 1949.

4. *Billboard Magazine*, July 30, 1949; "Bob-lo Gets 382G for Detroit Land," *Billboard Magazine*, October 1, 1949. Club Bob-lo was the source of revenue that helped the Fletchers survive the long winter months between Bob-lo Island seasons. Bill Browning, perturbed that the city allowed the land to sit undeveloped for several years after the condemnation depriving them of revenues from Club Bob-lo, vowed to become involved with city politics and a part of decision making in the future. Bill Browning, interview, November 2003.

5. Chuck Bade, interview, July 2003. In 1955 Thomas Patton, Republic Steel president, replaced Troy Browning's name with his own on one of the ships. In 1957 the Wilson Marine Transit Company acquired the Republic iron ore contract, and Browning lost much of its business. Browning Steamship Lines was sold in 1965. Ever entrepreneurial, Browning Steamship Lines also had a Cuban merchant marine operation in the 1950s. They worked with the Batista government to set it up and lost $500,000 when Castro came into power.

6. J. Albin Jackman, ed., *Ahoy and Farewell: Twenty-fifth Anniversary of the Marine Historical Society of Detroit* (Grosse Ile, MI: Marine Historical Society of Detroit, 1969), 191.

7. Woody Herrala, interview, October 2003.

8. "Kiddieland Added to Bob-lo," *Billboard Magazine*, July 16, 1955; Bob-lo File, Burton Historical Collection, Detroit Public Library, Detroit, Michigan.

9. Bill Browning, interview, December 2004. A note on the numbers: Bill Browning counted total passengers on boats from both Detroit and Amherstburg (and occasionally other places). He then subtracted 60,000 per season from those numbers for Detroit charters that did not go to the island. He estimates that, for the 1960s and 1970s, they averaged 530,000 from Detroit and 150,000 from Amherstburg. With 60,000 subtracted for charters, average attendance for Bob-lo Island would have then been in the 620,000 range.

10. Chuck Bade, interview, July 2003; Woody Herrala, interview, October 2003.

11. Elizabeth Thompson, interview, May 2004.

12. U.S. Army Corps of Engineers, *Essayons* (Washington, DC: Government Printing Office, 2002); *Our Downriver River* (Gibralter, MI: Rockne P. Smith, 1997). With the opening of the St. Lawrence Seaway, the Bob-lo lighthouse was decommissioned and placed under the responsibility of Fort Malden. Its light that had served mariners for over 120 years was replaced by automated beacons located on the White Sands.

13. "Business in 5% Gain at Detroit's Bob-lo," *Billboard Magazine,* September 9, 1957.

14. Lighthouse brochure, Marsh Collection Society.

15. Bill Browning, interview, November 2003.

16. Art Carter, interview, November 2004.

17. "Bob-lo Adds Train," *Billboard Magazine,* April 1958; *Billboard Magazine,* June 23, 1958; Ralph Browning, interview, November 2004.

18. "Special Days Aid Grosses at Bob-lo," *Billboard Magazine,* July 14, 1958.

19. Ibid.; "Detroit Area up 10 Percent," *Billboard Magazine,* July 21, 1958.

20. U.S. Coast Guard Proceedings, September 14, 1959, and August 10, 1960; "*Canadiana* Hits Bridge in Toledo," *Windsor (ON) Star,* August 6, 1958.

21. Denise Bondy, interview, July 2003.

22. Bill Browning, interview, August 2003.

23. Ibid.

24. "Bob-lo Opens on Holiday," *Billboard Magazine,* May 18, 1959.

25. Catherine Clapsaddle, Mary Beth Vitale, Art Herrala, Bill Browning, Ralph Browning, interviews, September and November 2003.

26. "OK Bob-lo Dock for '62," *Amusement Business,* January 6, 1962; "Bob-lo Dock May Go," *Amusement Business,* October 6, 1962.

27. Fred Smitka, interview, July 2003.

28. http://www.thebig8.net/sounds.html, courtesy of Mark Elliott.

29. *Detroit Free Press,* May 10, 1964. The 1949 season attendance was probably hampered by the fact that there were serious doubts that Bob-lo would even operate until virtually the last minute. There was little time to generate group sales under those circumstances.

30. Bob-lo promotional flyer, Dossin Museum.

31. *Amusement Business,* September 19, 1964. Given the formula discussed in note 9, this would put the total well over six hundred thousand.

32. David A. Carson, *Grit Noise and Revolution: The Birth of Detroit Rock and Roll* (Ann Arbor: University of Michigan Press, 2005), 77, 104.

33. Herb Colling, *Turning Points: The Detroit Riot of 1967: A Canadian Perspective* (Toronto: Natural Heritage Books, 2002), 175. While the Brownings did not discriminate against blacks as customers, neither did they solicit their patronage because they believed that excessive black patronage would result in a reduced white patronage and lower overall attendance. Black organizations and churches increasingly chartered the boats for moonlight cruises, reserving most Monday nights of the season. Bill Browning, interview, June 2003.

34. "Probe Likely in Bob-lo Death," *Windsor (ON) Daily Star,* August 26, 1965.

35. *Amusement Business,* August 5, 1967; Art Herrala, interview, October 2003; Bill Browning, interview, November 2003.

36. *Amusement Business,* August 24, 1968; "New Bob-lo Facilities Cost $1,000,000," *Windsor (ON) Star,* May 23, 1969.

37. Judith A. Adams, *The American Amusement Park Industry: A History of Technology and Thrills* (Boston: Twayne, 1991).

38. Philadelphia Toboggan Company to Bob-lo management, March 5, 1969, Charles J. Jacques Jr. Collection, Dossin Museum.

39. *Amusement Business,* May 3, 1969.

40. *Amusement Business,* May 9, 1970, and July 18, 1970.

41. "Concern Expressed Over Bob-lo Hiring Policy," *Windsor (ON) Star,* May 27, 1971; "Bob-lo Starts New Policy," *Amusement Business,* July 24, 1971.

42. "Detroit's Tiniest Princess Is Dead at 83," *Detroit Free Press,* October 30, 1968; "Captain Bob-lo Dies at 91," *Detroit Free Press,* December 20, 1974; Art Herrala, Bill Browning, and Ralph Browning, interviews, October and November, 2003.

43. "Bob-lo Goes P.O.P.," *Amusement Business,* April 7, 1973. See also *Great Lakes Red Book* (Cleveland: Penton, 1972).

44. *Windsor (ON) Star,* February 14, 1972.

45. *Monroe (MI) Evening News,* August 25, 1982.

46. "Bob-lo Offers New Features," *Detroit News,* April 18, 1974; Bill Browning, interview, November 2003.

47. Ibid.

48. "Ferry to Bob-lo Runs Aground," *Windsor (ON) Star,* July 10, 1974; Art Herrala, interview, November 2003.

49. "Mother, Child Hurt in Bob-lo Accident," *Windsor (ON) Star,* June 12, 1974.

50. Bill Browning, interview, November 2003.

51. "Big New Bob-lo Plan Unveiled," *Detroit News,* August 24, 1975.

52. *Amusement Business,* November 26, 1977.

53. Bill Browning, interview, November 2003.

54. Ted Diesbourg, interview, August 2003.

55. Bill Browning, interviews, June 2003 and November 2003.

56. *Windsor (ON) Star,* August 8, 1977.

57. "Accident Probed at Bob-lo," *Windsor (ON) Star,* July 14, 1978.

Chapter 7

1. Jeff Laderman, "We Almost Lost Bob-lo," *Detroit News Michigan Magazine,* May 9, 1982, 12.

2. Louis Cook, "When the Bob-lo Boats Almost Went Under," *Detroit Free Press,* May 25, 1980.

3. Laderman, "We Almost Lost Bob-lo."

4. *Amusement Business,* June 2, 1979.

5. Island of Bob-lo Company, news release, May 1980, Dossin Museum.

6. This increase drew complaints of price gouging from several Detroit City Council members who relied upon charters for election fundraisers over the years. The council threatened to hold up permission for site improvements to the Detroit dock unless charter rates were lowered. A compromise was reached when the company agreed to accept lower down payments for the charters with the balance to be paid from charter proceeds.

7. Laderman, "We Almost Lost Bob-lo."

8. "Too Much Too Soon for Bob-lo," *Amusement Business,* September 13, 1980.

9. Laderman, "We Almost Lost Bob-lo."

10. "Despite Problems, Bob-lo Future Looking Good," *Amusement Business,* March 27, 1982.

11. "Bob-lo Alien-Smuggling Ring Busted," *Detroit News,* November 16, 1982.

12. "Short-term Loans Would Bail Out Bob-lo," *Amusement Business,* October 9, 1982.

13. "Bob-lo Needs a Buyer," *Detroit Free Press,* November 28, 1982.

14. Price-Waterhouse (Canada), Bob-lo sales flyer, January 1983.

15. "Canadian Group Bids on Bob-lo," *Detroit News,* February 16, 1983.

16. "Michigan's AAA Has Plan to Make Bob-lo Even Better," *Windsor (ON) Star,* March 16, 1983.

17. Ibid.

18. Ibid.

19. "Court O.K.'s AAA Purchase of Bob-lo," *Amusement Business,* April 30, 1983.

20. Ibid.

21. Automobile Club of Michigan, news release, "Bob-lo Improvement Plan Announced," December 8, 1983, Dossin Museum.

22. Ibid.; "$2.3 Million Fix Up for Bob-lo," *Amherstburg (ON) Echo,* December 14, 1983.

23. Automobile Club of Michigan, news release, September 1984, Dossin Museum.

24. "Vekoma Coaster Highlights Bob-lo Upgrade," *Amusement Business,* February 23, 1985.

25. "Bomb Threat Against Bob-lo," *Detroit News,* August 11, 1985.

26. "Record Year at Bob-lo," *Amusement Business,* November 23, 1985; Ted Diesbourg, interview, July 2003.

27. "Fixing a Carousel," *Norwalk (OH) Reflector,* December 4, 1986.

28. *Detroit News,* August 14, 1987.

29. "Bob-lo Island Attendance Up," *Amusement Business,* October 31, 1987; *Detroit Monitor,* April 28, 1988.

30. "Broadcast Firm to Buy Bob-lo," *Detroit Free Press,* May 11, 1988; "Bob-lo Island Deal," *Amusement Business,* June 4, 1988.

31. Ibid.

32. "It Was Mayday on the Bob-lo Boat," *Windsor (ON) Star,* May 31, 1988; Art Herrala, interview, November 2003.

33. Bob-lo Island brochure, 1989.

34. "Old Amusement Ride to Be Auctioned," *Detroit Free Press,* February 5, 1990; "Carousel Sale Grosses More Than $860,000," *Amusement Business,* March 12, 1990.

35. "Unique Transportation System," *Amusement Business,* January 14, 1991.

36. "IBC Puts Bob-lo Up for Sale," *Amusement Business,* February 24, 1992.

37. Bob-lo Island promotional brochure, 1991.

38. Newspaper clipping, *Amherstburg (ON) Echo,* September 11, 1991, scrapbook, Marsh Collection Society.

39. "IBC Puts Bob-lo Up for Sale."

40. Ibid.

41. Ibid.

42. "Rough Time for Bob-lo," *National Amusement Park Historical Association News* 14, no. 2 (May 1992): 21.

43. Bob-lo Island brochure, 1992.

44. "Bob-lo's New Owners Await Final OK," *Amusement Business,* March 1, 1993.

45. "Bob-lo Island Auction Set," *Amusement Business,* November 30, 1992.

46. "A Tragic Ride for Bob-lo Dreamer," *Detroit Free Press,* August 11, 1997.

47. "Bob-lo's New Owners Await Final OK."

48. "Bob-lo Was Holiday's Hot Ticket," *Detroit Free Press,* July 9, 1993. Ted Diesbourg recalls large crowds over that weekend but believes that there were even larger crowds in the 1970s—up to eighteen thousand at one point. However, that was when the *Columbia* and the *Ste. Claire* transported ten thousand people round trip (including a moonlight to the island) on a full capacity day. That would mean the *Papoose* fleet would bring in an additional eight thousand from Amherstburg, a possibility given that they could transport about twelve hundred people per hour. Joe Lamour, who captained one of the Gibraltar boats in the 1990s remembers the Gibraltar dock capacity being about one thousand per hour with a forty-five-minute one-way run to the island, limited to about eight running hours per day for passenger delivery (leaving eight for passenger pickup)—a total of five thousand passengers. Diesbourg says the Amherstburg dock could handle up to twelve hundred people (optimal) per hour on its ten-minute run to the island. Under ideal circumstances, that dock could transport up to twelve thousand people in ten hours of runs, leaving only seven hours to get people back to the mainland, which is why there were some nights that they did not stop until 3 AM. In any case, crowds in the sixteen to eighteen thousand range would have depended upon perfect loading and unloading conditions for the entire day from both the Amherstburg and Gibraltar docks.

49. "Bob-lo Island Gets OK to Use U.S. Boats," *Detroit Free Press,* August 4, 1993.

50. "Boaters Bring Water to Bob-lo Resident," *Detroit Free Press,* August 17, 1993.

51. "Bob-lo to Close Gibraltar Dock," *Detroit Free Press,* September 14, 1993.

52. *Detroit News,* March 13, 1994; "A Tragic Ride for Bob-lo Dreamer."

53. "Bob-lo Island Is History," *Amusement Business,* February 28, 1994.

54. Ibid.

55. "Bob-lo Is No Longer Amusing," *Detroit Free Press,* March 8, 1994.

56. Ibid.

57. "A Tragic Ride for Bob-lo Dreamer."

Chapter 8

1. "New Owner Wants Bob-lo Visitors Back," *Detroit Free Press,* August 10, 1994.
2. Bois Blanc Island Resort Community brochure, 1997.
3. Bob-lo Island Resort sales sheet, 1997, author's collection.
4. "Bob-lo District Planned," *Detroit News,* June 27, 1999. Throughout the 1990s rumors had abounded about the fate of the large Bob-lo steamers *Columbia* and *Ste. Claire.* Promising headlines talked of various entrepreneurs who wanted to refurbish the vessels and bring them back to service on the river, but none of those plans came to fruition, and the boats found a nesting spot in the old Nicholson Dock in Ecorse.
5. The *Ste. Claire* was towed to Toledo by a Gaelic tug on September 11, 2001. The ship had been bought by a former Detroiter—now a Cleveland businesswoman—and her husband, who rescued the ninety-one-year-old vessel from the Nicholson docks with the intent of giving it a new life.
6. Newspaper clippings, *Amherstburg (ON) Echo,* July 16, 2002, August 6, 2002, and April 22, 2003, scrapbook, Marsh Collection Society.
7. Ontario Ministry of Environment, news release, "Fines Totalling $87,500 Handed down at Bob-lo Island," January 2, 2004.
8. Newspaper clipping, *Amherstburg (ON) Echo,* December 10, 2002, scrapbook, Marsh Collection Society; John and Mary Pandolfo, interview, December 2004.
9. "Town Won't Step In," *Amherstburg (ON) Echo,* April 22; "Debate On Ferry Continues," *Amherstburg (ON) Echo,* May 6; *Amherstburg (ON) Echo,* September 30, 2003; John and Mary Pandolfo, interview, December 2004.
10. "Major Investment for Bob-lo Island," *Amherstburg (ON) Echo,* December 23, 2003.
11. "KPMG of Toronto Appointed by Court," *Amherstburg (ON) Echo,* May 11, 2004.
12. "Amico Awarded Contract," *Amherstburg (ON) Echo,* August 3, 2004.
13. Ontario Superior Court Report, August 9, 2004, Marsh Collection Society.
14. "Big Plans For Bob-lo," *Windsor (ON) Star,* October 19, 2005.

Afterword

1. As of 2007, the Columbia has been bought by a Manhattan businessman who plans to restore her to service on the Hudson River. The *Ste. Claire* has been sold by her Cleveland-based owners to a Detroit physician who hopes to restore her to the Detroit River.
2. Maynard Hurst, interview, July 2003.
3. Ted Diesbourg, interview, August 2003.

NOTE ON SOURCES

For the geographical background I have used Ronald J. Mason, *Great Lakes Archaeology* (New York: Academic Press, 1981); Stanley J. Bolsenga and Charles E. Herdendorf, *Lake Erie and Lake St. Clair Handbook* (Detroit: Wayne State University Press, 1993); and *The Great Lakes: An Environmental Atlas and Resource Book* (Chicago: U.S. Environmental Protection Agency and Government of Canada, 1995).

For the human settlement and land use background, I have used Russell McKee, *Great Lakes Country* (New York: Crowell, 1966); Shari L. Dann and Brandon C. Schroeder, *The Life of the Lakes: A Guide to the Great Lakes Fishery* (Ann Arbor: Michigan Sea Grant College Program, 2003); Ernest J. LaJeunesse, *The Windsor Border Region, Canada's Southernmost Frontier: A Collection of Documents* (Toronto: University of Toronto Press, 1960); *The Michigan Pioneer and Historical Collection* (Washington, DC: Library of Congress, 1887) *Amherstburg, 1796–1996: The New Town on the Garrison Grounds, Book I* (Amherstburg, ON: Amherstburg Bicentennial Book Committee, 1996); Clark Everett, *Land Use History of the Canadian Detroit River Islands* (London, ON: University of Western Ontario, 1975); W. H. Smith, "Huron Village of the Island of Bois Blanc," in *Canada, Past, Present and Future* (Toronto: T. Maclear, 1851); David Botsford, "The History of Bois Blanc Island" *Ontario History Magazine* (Summer 1955); Daniel G. Hill, *The Freedom-Seekers: Blacks in Early Canada* (Toronto: Stoddart, 1992); Dennis Carter-Edwards, *Fort Malden: A Structural Narrative History, 1796–1976*, vol. 1 (n.p.: Parks Canada, 1980); John H. Hartig, ed., *Honoring Our Detroit River: Caring for Our Home* (Detroit: Wayne State University Press, 2003); and the Walpole Island First Nation's Web site, http://www.bkejwanong.com.

For recent history (from 1860 forward), I have used David Beasley, *Alexander McKee and the Heyday of the American Theater* (Waterloo, ON: Laurier University Press, 2004); Gordon Bugbee, "Stars on the River" Steamboat Bill Magazine (Winter 2001): 256–93; Gordon Bugbee, "Ballroom Boats" Telescope Magazine (May 2000); Michael Dixon, *When Detroit Rode the Waves* (Grosse Pointe, MI: Mervue, 2001); William Oxford, *The Ferry Steamers: The Story of the Detroit-Windsor Ferry Boats* (Toronto: Boston Mills, 2002); Rockne P. Smith, *Our Downriver River* (Gibraltar, MI: privately published, 1997); U.S. Army Corps of Engineers, *Essayons* (Washington, DC: Government Printing Office, 2002); William Moffett, *The Story of Bob-lo* (Detroit: Bob-lo Excursion Company, 1943); and Judith A. Adams, *The American Amusement Park Industry: A History of Technology and Thrills* (Boston: Twayne, 1991).

I must also recognize here the archives of the Burton Historical Society of the Detroit Public Library, the Windsor Public Library, the Letty Library of the University of Windsor, the Marsh Collection of Amherstburg, and the Dossin Great Lakes Museum of the Detroit Historical Museum on Belle Isle. The Dossin Collection includes the scrapbooks of the Detroit, Belle Isle, and Windsor Ferry Company, 1896–1907, the minutes of the Ferry Company, 1910–38, the Ferry Company ledgers, 1924–36, a significant photo archive, and a Bob-lo file.

INDEX